Telling Stories

TO
CHILDREN

Telling Stories

TO

CHILDREN

BY SYLVIA ZISKIND

NEW YORK

THE H.W. WILSON COMPANY

1976

PRINTED IN THE UNITED STATES OF AMERICA

Library of Congress Cataloging in Publication Data

Ziskind, Sylvia, 1906-
   Telling stories to children.

   Bibliography: p.
   Includes index.
   1. Story-telling.   I.   Title.
   LB1042.Z57   372.6'4   75-42003
   ISBN 0-8242-0588-X

LB
1042
.Z57

ACKNOWLEDGMENTS

The author wishes to thank the following for permission to quote material from their books: Coward, McCann & Geoghegan, Inc., for the opening lines of "Thorn Rose" from *More Tales from Grimm* by Wanda Gág, copyright 1947 by the estate of Wanda Gág. Reprinted by permission of Coward, McCann & Geoghegan, Inc.; Doubleday & Company, Inc., for "Open House," copyright 1941 by Theodore Roethke and "The Waking," copyright 1953 by Theodore Roethke, both from *The Collected Poems of Theodore Roethke*. Reprinted by permission of Doubleday & Company, Inc.; Doubleday & Company, Inc., for the haiku verse by Issa from *An Introduction to Haiku* by Harold G. Henderson, copyright ©1958 by Harold G. Henderson. Reprinted by permission of Doubleday & Company, Inc.; Houghton Mifflin Company, Inc., for the lines from "Ars Poetica" by Archibald MacLeish from *Collected Poems 1917–1952* by Archibald MacLeish. Reprinted by permission of Houghton Mifflin Company; Alfred A. Knopf, Inc., for "April Rain Song" and "The Dream Keeper" by Langston Hughes, both from *Don't You Turn Back* by Langston Hughes, copyright 1932 by Alfred A. Knopf, Inc., renewed 1960 by Langston Hughes. Reprinted by permission of the publisher; E. P. Dutton for "Spring Rain" by Marchette Chute from *Around and About* by Marchette Chute, copyright ©1957 by E. P. Dutton & Co., Inc., and reprinted with their permission;

E. P. Dutton for "Galoshes" by Rhoda Bacmeister from *Stories to Begin On* by Rhoda Bacmeister, copyright 1940 by E. P. Dutton, renewal ©1968 by Rhoda W. Bacmeister. Reprinted by permission of the publishers, E. P. Dutton & Co., Inc.; E. P. Dutton for "Wind on the Hill" by A. A. Milne from *Now We Are Six* by A. A. Milne, copyright 1927 by E. P. Dutton & Co., renewal ©1955 by A. A. Milne. Reprinted by permission of the publishers, E. P. Dutton & Co., Inc.; The Literary Trustees of Walter de la Mare and The Society of Authors as their representative for "Tired Tim" and "Some One" by Walter de la Mare; Doubleday & Company, Inc., for "Regents Park" by Rose Fyleman from *Gay Go Up* by Rose Fyleman, copyright 1929, 1930 by Doubleday and Company, Inc. Reprinted by permission of Doubleday & Company, Inc.; Simon & Schuster, Inc., for "Mountains" by Sakai Akiko from *There Are Two Lives*, Richard Lewis, ed., translated by Haruna Kimura, ©1970 by Richard Lewis and Haruna Kimura, reprinted by permission of Simon & Schuster, Children's Book Division; Simon & Schuster, Inc., for "Rain" by Leila Heron from *Miracles: Poems by Children of the English-Speaking World*, Richard Lewis, ed. ©1966 by Richard Lewis. Reprinted by permission of Simon & Schuster; Denise Embry for her poem "Thoughts of a Child"; Holt, Rinehart and Winston for "Talking" by Michael Goode and "Life" by Paul Goggins from *The Voice of the Children*, collected by June Jordan and Terri Bush, copyright ©1968, 1969, 1970 by The Voice of the Children, Inc. Reprinted by permission of Holt, Rinehart and Winston, Publishers; Holt, Rinehart and Winston for 2 haiku poems from *Come Along!* by Rebecca Caudill, copyright ©1969 by Rebecca Caudill. Reprinted by permission of Holt, Rinehart and Winston, Publishers; Holt, Rinehart and Winston for a line from a January 1916 letter by Robert Frost from *Letters of Robert Frost to Louis Untermeyer*, copyright ©1963 by Louis Untermeyer and Holt, Rinehart and Winston. Reprinted by permission of Holt, Rinehart and Winston, Publishers; Voice of the Children, Inc., for "The City" by Juanita Bryant, copyright ©1968 by Voice of the Children, Inc. Reprinted by permission of the author; Simon & Schuster for "The Fire Hydrant" by Ricky Preiskel from *Journeys*, copyright ©1969 by Richard Lewis. Reprinted by permission of Simon & Schuster, Inc.; J. B. Lippincott for "The Night Will Never Stay" by Eleanor Farjeon from *Poems for Children* by Eleanor Farjeon, copyright 1951 by Eleanor Farjeon. Reprinted by permission of J. B. Lippincott Company; J. B. Lippincott for "The Goblin" by Rose Fyleman from *Picture Rhymes from Foreign Lands* by Rose Fyleman. Copyright 1935, © renewed 1963 by Rose Fyleman. Reprinted by permission of J. B. Lippincott Company; Holt, Rinehart and Winston for "A Time to Talk" and "Fire and Ice" by Robert Frost from *The Poetry of Robert Frost* edited by Edward Connery Latham. Copyright 1916, 1923, © 1969 by Holt, Rinehart and Winston, Inc. Copyright 1944, 1951 by Robert Frost. Reprinted by permission of Holt, Rinehart and Winston, Publishers; Harcourt Brace Jovanovich, Inc., for "Fog" by Carl Sandburg from *Chicago Poems* by Carl Sandburg, copyright 1916, by Holt, Rinehart and Winston, Inc.; copyright, 1944 by Carl Sandburg. Reprinted by permission of Harcourt Brace Jovanovich, Inc.; Harcourt Brace Jovanovich, Inc., for "The Kite" by Harry Behn from *Windy Morning*, copyright, 1953 by Harry Behn. Reprinted by permission of Harcourt Brace Jovanovich, Inc.; Harcourt Brace Jovanovich for "Hallowe'en" by Harry Behn from *The Little Hill* by Harry

ACKNOWLEDGMENTS

Behn, copyright, 1949, by Harry Behn. Reprinted by permission of Harcourt Brace Jovanovich, Inc.; Thomas Y. Crowell for "A Bird" by Emily Dickinson from *The Poems of Emily Dickinson*, selected by Helen Plotz, copyright ©1964 by Helen Plotz; Alma J. Sarett for "The Four Little Foxes" by Lew Sarett from *Covenant with Earth; A Selection of the Poetry of Lew Sarett*. Edited and copyright, 1956, by Alma Johnson Sarett (Gainesville: University of Florida Press, 1956). Reprinted by permission of Mrs. Sarett; Indiana University Press for "For Children" by Gabriela Mistral from *Selected Poems of Gabriela Mistral*, translated by Langston Hughes, copyright ©1957 by Indiana University Press, Bloomington. Reprinted by permission of the publisher.

This book is dedicated with love to
Belinda,
Kevin, and
Allan

TABLE OF CONTENTS

RECENTLY, when I was telling the story "The Lass Who
Went Out at the Cry of Dawn" to sixth graders in a Chicano
school in Los Angeles, we were suddenly interrupted by the
persistent, staccato ringing of a fire alarm bell. Although it
was only a scheduled fire drill, the children, their teacher,
and I had to leave the building. I thought the break would
surely mark the end of the story hour. To my surprise and
delight, however, when the fire drill was over, the children
implored me to continue the tale from where I had left
off—the wicked wizard had just told the younger sister to
select her real sister from among seven identical statues!
The suspense of the story was strong enough to bridge the
bustle of our sudden departure and to restore to the children
their listening unity in a matter of seconds. Once again we
were caught up together in the mystery and excitement of
the tale, and we now had a strong bond between us. The
story was no longer mine alone; it belonged to my listeners
as well.

I have been telling stories for as long as I can remember
and under every possible circumstance. As a child, I amused
my younger brother with stories; I told tales to the children
at school; I remember the thrill of reciting poetry in the
school auditorium. While at college, I told stories every
Saturday morning to youngsters in the Los Angeles Public
Library. Both as a mother with children and as a grand-
mother with more children, I have always responded to the
plea, "Tell me a story." As a speech major at the university,

as a drama director in Washington, D.C., as a high school librarian in southern California, as a professor of children's literature, and as a community volunteer in the Reading Is Fundamental program, I have been an untiring and constant storyteller.

I do not know if my love of storytelling prompted me to pursue the study of speech and drama, or if my studies led me back to improve my storytelling. Whichever it was, I got a master's degree in speech arts and went on to teach and to act, all the while telling stories. I have long been interested in children's theater that encourages natural, creative dramatics instead of imitative, "show-off" theatricals. My experience in this field has enabled me to use poetry, choral speaking, and creative theater to enhance my own story hours and to show my students how to add these techniques to their storytelling experience.

As with all storytellers, I not only read all sorts of stories, but I listen to other storytellers. We learn much from each other. I remember how impressed I was when I visited the public square in Marrakesh, Morocco, and observed the professional storytellers holding their audiences enthralled. Every afternoon, as they have for hundreds of years, storytellers there have captivated their listeners with tales. I was drawn to one man, dressed in a long robe, with a little round cap on his head, and holding in his hand a small book, the pages of which were worn and yellowed with age with some loose from the binding. As he turned the pages from time to time, it was apparent that he scarcely needed a script to remind him of the events in his story, so much a part of him were the words and the characters. He sat down on a small stool occasionally, but mostly he stood or moved about in front of his attentive listeners. Old men, women, and children put age differences aside as they fused into a single audience. Even though I did not understand the man's words, I readily recognized that he practiced many of the principles and techniques of storytelling that I have written into this book.

Telling Stories to Children introduces practical means by which the reader can develop skill in the art of storytelling. I have tried to make the book simple enough to appeal to the totally inexperienced teller of stories; at the same time, I have indicated more advanced techniques and procedures for those who wish to become professional storytellers. It is my hope that parents, recreation workers, teachers, and librarians will all find helpful suggestions and guidelines to make them successful tellers of stories to children.

Chapter 1   SELECTING THE STORY

How and where does one begin to cultivate the art of storytelling? First, find a story that begs to be told. More accurately, find a story that begs you to tell it.

When Alice told the Queen she *could not* believe impossible things, the Queen replied, "I daresay you haven't had much practice . . . Why sometimes I've believed as many as six impossible things before breakfast."[1] If you are able to believe impossible things, you are ready to begin your search for a story to tell.

If, after a first reading, the story lingers in your thoughts and beckons you back, that is a good sign. It should evoke in you a warm reaction to its plot, its characters, and its style. Your genuine affinity to it is most important, for you alone must decide which, of all the stories in the world, are the best ones for you to learn and tell.

There are a great many stories that possess the magic power to transport young listeners from our mundane world of bells, buttons, and buzzers; of regimentation and conformity—into another world and another time, where dreams are more real than reality, where a mouse is sometimes more powerful than a lion and a lion is sometimes gentler than man, and where one can believe impossible things. My advice to the novice storyteller beginning the quest for a good story is to relax, read, and revel, and the impossible will become possible.

There are countless available collections of stories, and each collection has in it stories that someone, someplace, and sometime has found successful in the telling. The testimony of another collector of stories, however, carries with it no guarantee that his or her favorite stories will be the ones you want to tell. Each storyteller must scratch for his or her own food, and, as Dryden said, "He who would search for pearls must dive below."[2]

Once you think you have a story you like, you must test it on yourself. There is a very simple test that anyone can perform: just read the story aloud every day or even twice a day for a week to see how it wears. If you like it as much after having read it aloud six or seven times, it is a good story for you to begin to learn.

Just as you search for the story that pleases *you*, you must also search for a story that will please your audience. What kind of audience will it be? Will the children be accustomed listeners or will the experience of listening to stories be totally unknown to them? Will they be very young? Will they be in the middle years of childhood? Will they be older boys and girls approaching the sophistication of adolescence? Will they be a voluntary and eager group, or will they be a captive and wary audience? The grade level or age of your audience is not the only factor in the selection of stories; far more important are the interests, attitudes, and comprehension of the children.

One of the comforting things about a collection of books in a library is that the books are not graded! A ten-year-old can read a picture-storybook with unabashed pleasure, whereas a second- or third-grader who is a good reader is free to read anything his ability and motivation prompt him to choose. Fortunately, there are many stories that have universal appeal, stories that will delight the very young and amuse and interest older children too. I have attended a story hour planned expressly for small children during which a couple of teen-agers cagily stood on the outer edges of the group and listened with obvious interest.

Fathers and mothers who were themselves deprived of children's stories when they were small usually discover a new source of enjoyment when they read to their own children.

All of this is simply to say that categorizing children's stories for particular age groups is, at best, conjecture. Experimentation, experience, sensitivity to children's needs and likes—these are the best determiners of what is desirable in the process of selection. Still, with my concern for my audience uppermost in my mind, I have often caught myself classifying stories by "appropriate" age levels. All I can say is: be flexible, and remember that the device is convenient but not always very accurate.

In general, stories for very little children should be short, simple, and, of course, within the range of their comprehension and experience. Picture books with little or no text are good for beginners. One or two of these books and a well-illustrated Mother Goose can easily make a good "first" story hour for very small children.

After children have become accustomed to listening, picture-storybooks with somewhat fuller texts are ideal. They appeal both to the eyes and the ears, they offer a story with the storyteller's interpretation, and they prepare the children for listening to stories that have no accompanying pictures. Picture-storybooks must be selected with caution, however, for although some books have a picture-book format, they may also have a story line and text far too sophisticated or lengthy for small children. Any one of these characteristics in a book should bar its use. Among the many excellent picture books to begin with are *Bruno Munari's Zoo*, Wanda Gág's *Millions of Cats*, and Taro Yashima's *Umbrella*.

Even though picture books are still popular with five-, six-, and seven-year-olds, these children can also enjoy more complex plotting and can cope with more mature vocabularies. Examples of more advanced books that are easily grasped by children of this age group are two books by Virginia Burton, *Mike Mulligan and His Steam Shovel* and *The Little House*, Maurice Sendak's *Where the Wild Things Are*, and Gail Haley's *A Story, a Story*.

Children from seven to ten years generally like longer stories with dramatic action. Folk and fairy tales are especially good because of their strong plots, satisfying resolution of conflict, and characters with whom the children can empathize and identify. Even old favorites, such as Hans Christian Andersen's "The Emperor's New Clothes," are still enjoyed by this age group. So are tales like "Thorn Rose, or the Sleeping Beauty," "Jack and the Bean Stalk," and "Mollie Whuppie."

For children ten years old and over, you might well turn to the great Greek and Norse myths as retold by storytellers like Padraic Colum, Andrew Lang, and Dorothy Hosford; or to American folktales such as one finds in the *Jack Tales* by Richard Chase or in *Pecos Bill* by James C. Bowman; or to folktales of other lands, such as Armenian tales by Virginia A. Tashjian, Scottish tales by Sorche nic Leodhas, and Jewish tales as related by Isaac Bashevis Singer. Occasionally, it is good to tell one episode of a long story, thereby encouraging the youngsters to read the entire book. A thrilling story that lends itself to this kind of telling is James Ramsey Ullman's *Banner in the Sky*. A hilarious tale that has wide appeal for boys and girls is the doughnut episode in Robert McCloskey's *Homer Price*.

Once you have found a story and have tested it on yourself to see whether you like it well enough to learn it, you still must test it on an audience. Until you do this, you cannot be really sure just how much detail or description from the text should be retained in your retelling and which events might be deleted or simply summarized. Because stories are not learned for a single "performance" but become a permanent part of the storyteller's repertoire, the first, second, or third tellings may still be considered part of the "testing" process of selection.

I suggest that you search for several very short tales that can be used together or separately as the need arises. Obviously, short stories are easier to learn than long ones. Short stories help to develop a sense of timing and timeliness—both important factors in planning a story hour. A short story or two from your repertoire can always be tucked into a program that needs expanding or rounding out. If you are unsure of your audience—perhaps it includes children of different age groups or of different ethnic backgrounds—it is much safer to tell several very short stories than to attempt a long one that may appeal to a small portion of the listeners.

Because children are quick to recognize nonsensical situations and react good-naturedly to humor and absurdity, I suggest that your first stories involve mainly humorous plots and incongruous characters. Nonsense shared between storyteller and listener creates instant rapport. Examples of such stories that appeal to many age groups are "Master of All Masters," "The Little Cream Cheese," "The Peddler and His Caps," and "The Old Woman and the Pig." These stories show the technical perfection of the short story form. Each presents an impossible situation, in which the action builds suspensefully to a climax. The ending of each is rapid, unexpected, and satisfying, enabling the teller and the audience to laugh together at the outcome.

Not every tale in your bag should be funny, however. The listening child needs to hear many types of stories if he is to develop his own sensitivity to spoken language and to the written word. Therefore, some must be sad; some, delicate and fanciful; others, mysterious and a bit scary; and still others should be bold and dramatic. You can achieve a varied repertoire in time and with experience and careful selection.

Selection is, of course, the key. Libraries abound in story collections from which you can choose. A few of these collections have been mentioned in this chapter; many more are listed in Chapter VII. Browse through them because they are among the richest sources for the storyteller. Folktales, for instance, may well be named the unifier of races, for we find the same themes, the very same plots weaving in and out of vastly different cultures, depicting man's beliefs, strengths, and ideals as well as his foibles and superstitions. And there are new stories, too—stories that may, in their turn, become classics.

In your selection of stories, the range of your own background is singularly important. As a storyteller, you should cultivate an appreciation of literature in all its forms. The wise storyteller is familiar with adult literature as well as children's stories. If you have been moved by profound poetry, great drama, or other forms of creative expression, you will bring a richer self to the story hour. The storyteller of old brought history, tradition, and current news to his audience as well as romance and adventure. The storyteller of today should be no less informed and skilled. Thousands of stimuli reach out to the child in his often lonely and bewildering existence. You must be attuned to our modern world, fraught as it is with both stresses and challenges. The storyteller should bring his young listeners a sense of his or her own being and worth, a courage to strive and to grow, an assurance of friendship and love, and a sense of wonder and imagination. When stories are so presented, children will run from play to listen. Even grown-ups may pause, linger, and listen too.

NOTES FOR CHAPTER 1

1. Lewis Carroll, *Alice's Adventures in Wonderland and Through the Looking Glass, and What Alice Found There* (New York: Macmillan, 1963.
2. John Dryden, "All for Love; or, The World Well Lost," in *Twelve Famous Plays of the Restoration and Eighteenth Century*, compiled by Bennett A. Cerf and Donald S. Klopfer (New York: Modern Library, 1933), Prologue.

Chapter 2   LEARNING THE STORY

You have learned a story only when it is all yours and you have become part of it. After you have chosen it, get to know each character as an old friend. You can then bring these old friends together with new friends in your audience. You have only a few points of identification—names, descriptive terms, actions, and moods—and you must convey them quickly. The more real the story is to you—that is, the more you know about the characters, their traits, and their behavior—the easier will be the telling. So reread the story, and meditate upon its people, its plot, its appealing language, until you feel that you can know no more about it. Rehearse the telling until you feel that the characters are certain to appear as you want them to. If you are reading poetry, study its spirit, its rhythm, its meaning, and then read or speak it aloud until you believe the listeners will hear it as you do. You and the story, when learned, should be one.

I have a few aids for the learning of a story. These are suggestions on what to notice, what to memorize, how to record things to be remembered, and how to refresh your memory. I do not have a magic formula. Your own personality must dictate the most effective way for you to learn a story. However, with the confidence that it may help you, too, I will describe how I and other storytellers have learned stories.

You have begun the learning process in your selection of the story. Note why it appeals to you, why you think it will charm others, who will be most receptive to it, and under what circumstances you might best use it. As you continue to test the story by reading it aloud from beginning to end, getting to know it intimately, you may see it in a new light. You will, in the very reading, observe the outstanding qualities and characteristics of the story. You will begin to take the people of the story and their actions into your mind and your heart, and your imagination will begin to tell you how you might present them to listeners.

Early along the way of learning, you should record what you must remember about the story. This can be done by means of a card file or a loose-leaf notebook. In either case, the storytelling file is an ongoing project and will expand as your repertoire develops.

I will describe the card file first and then the notebook arrangement.

I suggest the use of large cards, 4×6 or even 5×8, in order to avoid cramped or crowded writing. On one side of the card, write the name of the story; its author if known; the collection in which it is available; and the compiler, publisher, and date of publication. Indicate also the age group for which you think the story is best suited, the length of time it takes you to tell it, and any comments regarding it that you think may be helpful in future tellings.

The reverse side of the card becomes your "prompt book." I think it is desirable to record the first two or three sentences of the story and its ending; the identification of the characters; any refrains or unusual expressions used by the author; and, most important of all, the exact sequence of events.

The card system can easily be illustrated by the use of two simple stories, "Master of All Masters" and "The Little Cream Cheese."

MASTER OF ALL MASTERS
(author unknown)

A girl once went to the fair to hire herself for servant. At last a funny-looking old gentleman engaged her, and took her home to his house. When she got there, he told her that he had something to teach her, for that in his house he had his own names for things.

He said to her: "What will you call me?"

"Master or mister, or whatever you please, sir," says she.

He said: "You must call me 'master of all masters.' And what would you call this?" pointing to his bed.

"Bed or couch, or whatever you please, sir."

"No, that's my 'barnacle.' And what do you call these?" said he pointing to his pantaloons.

"Breeches or trousers, or whatever you please, sir."

"You must call them 'squibs and crackers.' And what would you call her?" pointing to the cat.

"Cat or kit, or whatever you please, sir."

"You must call her 'white-faced simminy.' And this now," showing the fire, "what would you call this?"

"Fire or flame, or whatever you please, sir."

"You must call it 'hot cockalorum,' and what this?" he went on, pointing to the water.

"Water or wet, or whatever you please, sir."

"No, 'pondalorum' is its name. And what do you call all this?" asked he as he pointed to the house.

"House or cottage, or whatever you please, sir,"

"You must call it 'high topper mountain.' "

That very night the servant woke her master up in a fright and said: "Master of all masters, get out of your barnacle and put on your squibs and crackers. For white-faced simminy has got a spark of hot cockalorum on its

tail, and unless you get some pondalorum high topper
mountain will be all on hot cockalorum."
That's all.

Master of All Masters   Very short

      in

Jacobs, Joseph. English Folk and Fairy Tales...

    Illus. by John D. Batten. Third ed., revised.

N.Y., G.P. Putnam's Sons. (n.d.)

Of interest to 6 - 12 year olds.

Must remember exact names for each thing.

      "Master of All Masters"

A girl once went to the fair to hire herself
for servant. At last a funny little old gentleman engaged her.

His special names for things:

Man asks	Girl says	Man says
Himself	Master or mister	Master of all masters
The bed	bed or couch	barnacle
pantaloons	breeches or pan-taloons	squibs and crackers
The cat	cat or kitten	white-faced simminy
Fire	fire or flame	hot cockalorum
Water	water or wet	pondalorum
House	house or cottage	high topper mountain

That night the young girl ran to her master's
door and knocked loudly. She shouted, "Master of all masters, get out of your barnacle
and put on your squibs and crackers. For
White-Faced Simminy has got a spark of hot
cockalorum on its tail, and unless you get
some pondalorum high topper mountain will be
all on hot cockalorum...." That's all.

11

THE LITTLE CREAM CHEESE

By Florence Botsford

Once upon a time there was a little girl named Matilda, who had nothing to eat. A peasant woman gave her a little cream cheese in a basket.

But Matilda did not like cream cheese. In fact she hated it so much that she would rather wash clothes in the river than take even one little taste.

So she made a crown out of long fern leaves and bound it around her head. She put the cheese in the crown and started to the marketplace to sell the little cream cheese.

As she was walking down the hill she thought, "Today I will go to the city and sell the cream cheese for a penny. With the penny I will buy two eggs. When the eggs are hatched, I will have two chickens. When they grow big enough, I will sell them and buy a lamb. When the lamb grows to be a big sheep, I will sell it and buy a calf. When the calf is big and fat, I will sell it and buy a colt. When the colt grows to be a horse, I will sell it and buy a lovely castle with a nice balcony in the front.

"There I will sit in a comfortable chair, taking my ease, and all the neighbors will pass by and say, 'How do you do, Lady Matilda.'

"But I will not take the trouble to answer such common people. I will just make them a grand bow like this"—and as Matilda bent over to make a low bow, the little cream cheese fell in the mud, and that was the end of her castle in the air—and—and—and—wasn't she hungry!

Although the notations on the cards should be brief, they will be most useful if they contain everything that you need to make the storytelling complete. For lengthy stories, you may require two cards.

The Little Cream Cheese   Very short

by Florence Botsford   2-3 minutes

in

Harper, Wilhelmina, Comp.   The Gunniwolf and Other Merry Tales.

    Phila., David McKay, 1936

Of interest to 5-10 year olds

Must remember sequence of items

Once upon a time there was a little girl named Matilda, who had nothing to eat. A peasant woman gave her a little cream cheese in a basket. Matilda didn't like cream cheese. Decided to sell it in the market place.

Made a crown of ferns and placed cheese in the crown on her head.
Thinks:

sell cheese	1 penny
buy 2 eggs	2 chickens
sell chickens	a lamb
sell sheep	a calf
sell cow	a colt
sell horse	a lovely castle

The people will say, "How do you do, Lady Matilda." But she won't answer. She will just make a grand, low bow - like this...

The little cheese fell in the mud, and that was the end of her castle in the air... and - wasn't she hungry!

You must decide on the arrangement of the cards. They can be grouped by title or author in alphabetical order or by subject heading or type of story or by suitable age groups. Whichever arrangement you choose, the important thing is to be consistent. You may find it expedient to list the story under two headings and have a cross-reference from one heading to another. For example, "Master of All Masters" might be filed under Humorous Stories, Silly Stories, or Very Short Stories, by title, as here, or by author if known. A cross-reference from one or more of these headings would refer you to the heading under which you have actually filed the story card. See the following example of such a cross-reference card.

```
                        Very Short Stories, See
        Master of All Masters
        The Little Cream Cheese
        The Little Dog
        The Sweet Porridge
        Lazy Jack
        Why the Bear Is Stumpy-Tailed
        The Town Mouse and the Country Mouse
```

In addition to using cards for stories you have chosen to learn, you may find it helpful to include names of stories you might want to consider at some future time. These cards may be labeled "Stories to Read and Test." Be sure to list all pertinent information about the collection in which you found the story, so that you can locate it with ease if and when you want to reread it. Such a card would look like the one in the following illustration.

```
                  Read and Test
THE TONGUE-CUT SPARROW, (Adapted by Shitakiri Suzume).  9 pages
      in
         Uchida, Yoshiko.  The Dancing Kettle and Other
                  Japanese Folk Tales.  Illus. by Richard C. Jones.
                  N.Y., Harcourt, 1949.

THE SELFISH GIANT, by Oscar Wilde.                       10 pages
      in
         Wilde, Oscar.  The Happy Prince and Other Tales.
         Illus. by Walter Crane and Jacomb Hood... N.Y.,
         Legacy Press, 1967.

THE FISHERMAN AND HIS WIFE, a folk tale.                 13 pages
      in
         Tales from Grimm, translated and illustrated by
            Wanda Gág.  N.Y., Coward-McCann, 1936.
```

An alternative to the card file is a loose-leaf notebook collection. This permits you to make a typed copy of the entire story. If you choose this plan, the notebook then becomes your personal anthology of the stories in your repertoire. As with the card file, the stories can be grouped in various ways: alphabetically by author or title, by subject, by type of story, that is, Humorous, Folktales, and so on, or by appropriate age or grade level. You must decide on the most practical and helpful arrangement for you. If you compile such an "anthology," be sure that you list at the top of the first page of each story the bibliographical data and information that were suggested for the card.

In the sample pages that follow, "Thorn Rose" is filed under its title within the group of Folktales, German. A cross-reference to it might be found under Romantic Stories, Fairy Tales, or All Ages.

Folktales, German

"Thorn Rose, the Sleeping Beauty"
in
Gág, Wanda. *More Tales From Grimm.* Freely translated and illustrated by Wanda Gág. New York, Coward McCann, 1947.
Of interest to children in the middle grades, 4–6.
Telling time: 10 minutes.

Note that the written version of this folk or fairy tale first appeared in France in 1697 in the famous collection by Charles Perrault entitled *Contes de ma mère l'Oye* ("Tales of My Mother Goose"). However, the Grimm brothers recorded it as a tale they encountered much later in Germany. Because it is their version I tell, I have arbitrarily included it in this section of Folktales, German.

Once upon a time—oh, that was many years ago—there lived a King and Queen who said every day, "Alas, if we only had a child!" But year after year passed by and still their wish was not granted.

Now it happened that one day as the Queen was bathing in a pool, a frog said to her, "Your wish will soon be granted. Before the year is up a daughter shall be born to you . . ."

And what the frog promised came true. Within the year a daughter was born, a child so wondrously beautiful that the . . .[1]

Folktales, German   Thorn Rose   Study Notes
Sequence of Events
1. King and Queen want a child; daughter is born; both overjoyed.
2. Splendid feast celebration; 12 Wise Women invited; not the 13th.
3. 11 W.W. bestow gifts; 13th enters and proclaims, "On her 15th birthday, the princess will prick her finger on a spindle and fall lifeless to the floor." She stalks out.
4. 12th W.W. cannot undo the curse but softens it: instead of death, princess will sleep for 100 years. King orders all spinning wheels in the kingdom burned.
5. Years pass, wishes of W.W. come true: princess lovely.
6. On 15th birthday, K. and Q. away; princess discovers old woman spinning in a tiny room of tower; tries to hold spindle but pricks finger and falls lifeless on bed. Deep sleep.
7. Everyone and everything in castle falls asleep: K. and Q. against thrones, lords, ladies of court: outside—animals, ducks, geese, chickens, doves on tower; inside—flies, fire on hearth, meat on spit, cook, skullery boy, maid; outside—breeze, trees, flowers, all asleep, *except* one thing: hedge of thorns that covers entire castle.
8. Years pass; legend of Thorn Rose, Sleeping Beauty lives on.
9. 100 years to the day, young prince arrives, determines to seek the sleeping beauty; hedge parts; he enters; dead silence; sees everyone asleep; searches for princess; finds her at last; kisses her and the spell is broken.

10. Together they go through the castle; everyone and everything is awakening; all amazed; glad to be alive.

11. Prince and Princess fall in love; soon there is a celebration in honor of their wedding.

Words and phrases to remember:

The feast was celebrated with great pomp and splendor.
Gifts: virtue, beauty, riches . . .
Everyone was shocked, and a dead silence fell upon the company.
The princess grew up so beautiful, charming and clever, and so kind and modest besides, that none who saw her could help loving her.
Upstairs and downstairs . . . peeping into halls and bedchambers and closets as the fancy took her.
The winding stairway, the old door, and a rusty key stuck in its lock; she turned the key and the door sprang open.
The old woman busily spinning flax; "Good day, little old mother," said the Princess. "What is it you are doing there?" "I am spinning," said the woman, nodding her head as she worked. "But what is spinning, and what is that thing which whirls around so merrily?" . . . "Let me try it too". . .
As soon as she touched it the curse of the 13th W.W. went into effect.
A deep, deep sleep.
All fell asleep just as they stood or walked or lay. On the roof the doves tucked their little heads under their wings and slept, and in the castle, the flies on the walls—yes, even the fire flaring and flickering on the hearth—became dead and still, and slept like all the rest. The meat stopped roasting on the spit, and the

cook, who was about to box the scullery boy's ears for
some mistake he had made, let him go and went to
sleep . . .
Outdoors . . . the wind ceased blowing, in the gardens the
flowers drowsily closed their petals, and on the trees
every leaf hung motionless . . .

Another section in the notebook would include poetry. In
the poetry section, the typed copies of poems may be arranged according to author, title, or subject. At the top of the
page, any suggestions regarding the use of the poem can be
noted, particularly if it can be used effectively with a specific
story.

A poetry entry in the notebook file might look like this:

Poetry   Older Boys and Girls
    Jiménez, Juan Ramón. *Platero and I.* Translated by
      Eloise Roach. Austin: University of Texas Press,
      1957.
    Very beautiful, poetic prose about the poet's little
    donkey. Must be introduced carefully. Sensitive,
    beautiful, and loving.

The text of the poem should follow. If you own the printed
book and plan to read from it, then instead of copying the
selection, you can simply list in your notebook the page
numbers of the book.

An entry for a poetry anthology might look like this:

Poetry   Small Children
    Geismer, Barbara Peck. *Very Young Verses.* Selected
      by B. P. Geismer and Antoinette Brown Suter. Bos-
      ton: Houghton Mifflin, 1948.
    A collection of delightful verses easy to understand
    and easy to read or speak.

Copy one or more of the poems that you find useful or list the pages of the poems you would read.

Poetry can also be grouped under such subject headings as Animals, Ocean, Children, and Nonsense; and under such age-level headings as Preschool, Older Boys and Girls, and All Ages.

Keeping records may seem unnecessarily burdensome if you are a novice storyteller, but veterans in this field will attest to its practical value. Story collections are sometimes elusive and hard to find, but if you have your notes from an earlier "telling," you will not need to find the book. You will be able to reconstruct the story from your cards, or you will be able to reread it in its entirety from your own notebook.

One pitfall in storytelling that must be avoided is the repetition of common terms in a way that is, at best, uninteresting and, at worst, boring. A character may be a beautiful princess, but instead of referring to her again and again as the "beautiful princess," try referring to her in different ways that contribute variety to your style and heighten and accentuate her image. Call her the "wondrous princess," the "charming and graceful young princess," "the king's daughter—always kind and courteous," "the shining, golden-haired princess," or use other expressions that denote loveliness and wonder. If the author's words are better than yours—as well they may be—write them on your card or in your notebook, and memorize them. If they are not natural or easy for you to say or remember, make your own list of synonyms, phrases, and expressions.

Consciously and deliberately, increase and enrich your speaking vocabulary. Poverty of language does not become the storyteller. Only through his own word richness can he recreate stories that sparkle and live for his listeners. So, form the dictionary habit, and use Roget's *Thesaurus*.

Sometimes storytellers feel compelled to memorize every story exactly as it was written by the author. Some stories should be so memorized whereas other stories can be told with more animation and intimacy when the author's words are not memorized.

I like to explain which stories should be memorized by quoting six lines from one of my favorite poets, Theodore Roethke. In his poem "Open House," he says in the second verse,

> My truths are all foreknown,
> This anguish self-revealed.
> I'm naked to the bone
> With nakedness my shield.
> Myself is what I wear:
> I keep the spirit spare.[2]

Some stories are "naked to the bone." There is no outer fleshiness of superfluous words. The tale is revealed through the sparing use of carefully selected language. Just as pebbles in a stream get washed smooth and clean through years of rolling and tossing, so some stories become pure and clear through years of telling and retelling. In such stories, every word in the tale becomes a necessary link to every other word, and the artistry of the story is lost if the words or their arrangement are changed. Memorization is recommended, therefore, for the story that would lose its raison d'être, its identity, its truth, if the words were changed. One *must* memorize Ludwig Bemelmans' *Madeline* and "The Three Billy-Goats-Gruff." The first is in metered verse, which demands memorization; the second is an example of a story the language of which is spare and superbly enunciated. It would be detrimental to the story to attempt superflous embroidery.

Learn the story by heart, not by rote. There is a difference. The one makes the story your very own through a gradual melding between the story and you; the other makes it yours, but in a mechanical way, disciplined, but unfeeling. Something happens as you live with a story during the learning period; an invisible catalyst is at work. The story shifts from the printed pages in a book to something that becomes a very real part of you. Perhaps it is unconscious memorization; perhaps you memorize your own words as you practice telling it. Whichever it is, the story becomes so much your own that you will find yourself telling it exactly the same way each time you retell it. Even after a lapse of months, during which time you do not think of the story, a quick rereading of your notes or the story itself will bring it back to you, and again you will tell it exactly as you had learned it. The inflection, the emphasis on certain words, the timing, and the words themselves, somehow imprinted on your memory, will be at your command.

Memorization, if achieved this way, will not be apparent. It will retain spontaneity and freshness, two most important attributes of storytelling.

Even in a story that does not demand verbatim memorization, one should still memorize certain parts of it: its beginning and ending; the names of people and places; refrains or pertinent expressions; and, beyond a doubt, the exact sequence of events.

This method of learning a story will also help to determine how much is to be memorized. I recently learned the superbly illustrated story "One Fine Day" by Nonny Hogrogian. On the surface, it is another folktale that builds upon repetition very much like "The Old Woman and the Pig" or "This Is the House That Jack Built." But as I lived with it, I realized Miss

Hogrogian, in her retelling of the Armenian tale, had achieved a welcome variety. After the woman chops off the fox's tail because he drank her milk, he goes to the cow, the fields, the stream, the maiden, the peddler, the hen, and the miller. He wants something from each, but each of his requests is worded differently: he begs, he asks, he pleads, he coaxes, he cries, and he becomes desperate. The refrains are similar but not identical. As I read the story and experienced the flow of the language, I felt ever more strongly that the author's words were exactly the right words to use. I felt comfortable with her words, and soon they became my words. There is always a little annoying uncertainty during the learning period when I grope for the author's words. At that point, I find it helpful to sit down and concentrate on the uncertain parts and write them in my notebook. The actual, physical process of writing words and phrases seems to help record them in my memory. It also helps me to select which words and expressions I feel I should remember.

Memorizing the beginning and the ending of a story gives the storyteller a framework in which to build the events that transpire. The beginning establishes the characters, the situation, and the problem. It is comforting to have all this on the tip of your tongue. As you begin to tell your story, you may still be in the process of assessing your audience or adjusting to a new situation; so it is certainly no time to ad-lib. If you have the author's words well in mind, you will get off to a good start.

The ending is a winding down of the plot, a resolution of the problem. The author's ending is usually brief, to the point, and final. It is not necessary to add embellishments.

If you know the beginning, the ending, and the exact sequence of events, you are well on your way to knowing the story. Add to this the author's refrains, expressions, names, and some of his descriptive passages, and you are ready to try telling it to an audience.

Whether a story is to be memorized or not, the method for learning is always the same. Read it aloud from start to finish. Relax and revel in it. If you are interrupted in the middle, do not go back to the beginning when you resume; pick it up where you left off and continue through to the end. And repeat this until the story is a part of you. You must know it as well as you know the story of your life. And you must feel it as if it were an important episode of your own life.

Learning a story proceeds through rehearsals and sometimes through actual storytelling performances too. The rehearsal is a testing and verification of how well you have learned the story. The interruption of a telephone or the entrance of a person into the room and your ability to go on as though nothing had happened will prove you have learned the story.

If you have a tape recorder, try taping your telling of the story.

Hear yourself as others hear you. This has the dual value of helping you to learn the story and experience critically your own voice, speech, tempo, emphasis, and inflection.

In addition to using a tape recorder, watch yourself in the mirror as you practice telling the story. See yourself as others see you.

Try telling the story to a member of your family—a child preferably or a friend who will give you an honest reaction. This practice telling may indicate necessary cuts or explanations that will enhance your eventual performance before a real audience.

Once you have learned the story and practiced it until you

feel ready to tell it, you should feel comfortable and confident. If you do, the children in your audience will be comfortable and attentive too.

NOTES FOR CHAPTER 2

1. Wanda Gág, *More Tales From Grimm* (New York: Coward McCann, 1947).
2. Theodore Roethke, *The Collected Poems of Theodore Roethke* (New York: Doubleday & Co., Inc. 1966).

Chapter 3 MASTERING TECHNIQUE

Everybody likes to tell a story. Little children do it effortlessly. Great artists do it with native talent and years of practice. Somewhere in between stand you and I. A little attention to certain techniques and continual effort can make better storytellers of us all.

There are ways to improve one's ability to tell a story. These are matters of voice, diction, dialects, posture, and demeanor. There is also the use of props or picture books. However you find you can improve your performance, it will require, as always, preparation and rehearsal for the all-important moment of performance.

Voice Improvement

An essential of good storytelling is an expressive voice. Although some voices are tonally more pleasing than others, all voices can be expressive, and you can improve your voice to its maximum potential. You need variety in range and volume and must avoid sounding forced or strained. Your emphasis should be appropriate to the words you are saying; and your inflections, meaningful. You should be able to project strongly without shouting or to create a quiet, cozy atmosphere while still being heard by everyone. Your speech—pronunciation and enunciation—should be correct, distinct, precise, and polished. These are qualities that can be cultivated.

Although this book does not explore in depth the anatomi-
cal factors involved in the production of voice and speech, a
few exercises are offered that will serve to initiate your
speech improvement. For further study and understanding,
as well as further exercises, see any of the good books on
voice or speech technique listed in Chapter 7.

The following exercises are recommended as a routine for
anyone who feels tense as the story hour approaches. Their
purpose is to relax and strengthen the muscles used in the
production of voice and the enunciation of speech sounds.

1. Swallow five times in succession.
2. Hum very softly with the lips barely touching. Vary the
   pitch—first high, then low, then in between. Alternate
   mm and *nn* sounds.
3. Close your eyes and let your head drop forward like a
   dead weight. Rotate your head to the right slowly, lazily.
   As you do this, droop your shoulders too. Repeat in the
   opposite direction. Open your eyes and swallow.
4. Yawn and stretch. Swallow.
5. Stand erect. Close your eyes. Let your head drop forward easily. Let your shoulders sag and your arms
   dangle. Bend easily at the waist, letting your torso
   droop. Lazily bend your knees and slide down to the
   floor in a relaxed heap. Swallow. Now slowly reverse the
   steps above. Lift your head, and open your eyes at the
   very end. Shake your arms and hands, then drop them
   to your sides, and relax.
6. Open your mouth wide, and speak the following sylla-
   bles softly, sustaining the vowels: *ma, zah, skah, hah.*
   Repeat.
7. Exaggerate the consonants, and make the vowels as
   round and full-bodied as possible. Watch yourself in the
   mirror. Open your mouth wide, and exercise your lip

muscles. Repeat: The road to Rome is rugged, round, and rough.

8. Repeat the humming, trying to get the *m* and *n* to vibrate through the nasal resonance chambers. While humming, open your mouth slowly, and let all the sound flow through your nose.

9. Sustain the *m* and *n*, as well as the vowels, in the following, and sing the words *moan, moon, mahn, mean, minn, munn.*

10. Articulate as precisely as you can the following:

   a. Peter Piper picked a peck of pickled peppers.
   b. Fee, fi, fo, fum.
   c. The large, brown ball.

11. *L* is a singing consonant as are *m* and *n*. Sustain the consonants as well as the vowels in the following: *loam, loan, loom, lahm, lumm, lean, line.*

12. The sound *ng* is made at the back of the nose and can be sustained as a singing sound. Sustain the *ng* as well as the other singing sounds in the following: *among, long, ding, dong; with a ring and a ding, and a ding dong dong.*

13. Looking in the mirror, try making faces with your lips. Push them forward, stretch them out to the sides, pucker them, and so forth. Then repeat with an exaggerated lip movement *baby, pope, pauper, bump, pomp, bright, prom, pram, proper, born, bring.* Repeat and pop the *p* and *b* sounds.

14. Read out loud *every day* even if it is only one paragraph. In your reading, strive to enunciate the consonants precisely and make the vowels round, rich, and full.

15. Make up your own word lists that call for different sounds such as

au	*ee*	*a oo*	*a ee*
p*au*city	re*trie*ve	m*ou*nd	m*i*ne
taunt	please	down	line
daughter	wheeze	found	time
naughty	reach	count	fine
sought	need	round	twine

Practice saying these aloud with clipped, sharp consonants and full vowel sounds.

One can hardly speak of voice improvement without mentioning breath control. Speech sounds are made by the vibration of the vocal cords as the air passes out of the lungs. The storyteller, like the actor or singer, must learn to conserve and control his outgoing breath in speech. Control is the key to strong, unforced, and well-modulated voice production. The books listed in Chapter 7 provide a good explanation of the intricacies of voice and sound.

Simply stated, the diaphragm, a muscle that lies between the thorax (chest cavity) and the stomach, expands and relaxes as one breathes in and out. The larger the air cavity, the more air rushes into it. So, the singer or speaker should fill his or her lungs to the fullest each time he or she inhales, then expel the air economically in a series of small exhalations. Many people inhale only tiny amounts of air during speech and then have to keep taking refills. If they filled their lungs adequately each time and learned to exhale small amounts of air, they would not need to gasp for more. With practice, one can inhale air so that the "breathy" sound is eliminated. The control of the outgoing air is accomplished by the control of the diaphragm. This can be mastered by anyone. Think of the diaphragm as the floor of the chest cavity. The expansion of the chest cavity stretches the diaphragm out to its tightest and largest dimension. As the air leaves the lungs, the thorax contracts, and the diaphragm relaxes and becomes smaller. The objective is to exhale slowly while speaking so as not to waste the breath.

Here are a few helpful exercises:

1. Inhale, placing one hand against the front of your rib cage and the other on your back, feeling the thorax expand. Breathe in silently and easily. Blow the air out in a long, steady, slow stream with your hands still on the rib cage or back. Feel the cavity get smaller.

2. Inhale again. This time, count from one to ten. Keep increasing the count to see how many numbers you can say on one, single breath.

3. Inhale. Blow on a candle flame, but do not extinguish it. Just keep it wavering as long as you can.

4. Inhale. Hold the edge of a card lightly to your slightly parted lips, and say "Ooooooh" slowly, producing a buzzing sound as the card vibrates.

5. Inhale. Expel all the air on one big "BOOM!" Inhale instantly and exhale on "GO!" Inhale again, and exhale on "STOP IN THE NAME OF THE LAW!"

6. Read a paragraph aloud, and see how far you can get without having to take a new breath. When you need to inhale, try doing it quickly, silently, and unobtrusively.

7. Read poetry; read Shakespeare; read prose. Always read *aloud*! Mark the selection with *p*'s to indicate where you can conveniently pause and take a breath.

These are simple exercises. Nonetheless, they are founded on scientific principles. They will not transform your voice overnight—weary hours of practice may be necessary—but they do work.

Poise Through Good Posture

Along with a good voice and clear enunciation, a storyteller should have poise and a pleasing presence.

Poise suggests balance and equilibrium; also composure, self-possession, and equanimity. Good posture is fundamental to poise. It does not matter if you sit on the floor or in a chair or if you stand while telling a story, so long as you are poised and comfortable. Look at yourself in the mirror, and see if you look comfortable, relaxed, and *graceful* when you sit on the floor. Do not hunch yourself over if you choose this position; keep your back straight. If you do not like what you see in the mirror, try standing, or sit on a chair or stool. Do whichever feels—and looks—comfortable for you. Remember that in an actual storytelling session, you must be close to your audience. A story is an intimate thing, and the teller should create an intimate atmosphere.

The following exercise will help you attain good posture and at the same time will take out any kinks or aches you may have between your shoulder blades:

1. Stand with your back against a closed door or wall that has no baseboard. Touch the wall with your heels, the calves of your legs, hips, shoulders, and head.
2. Stretch down with your fingertips. Turn the palms of your hands forward. Now let your head roll back slowly. This forces your shoulders slightly forward, away from the wall. Raise your head slowly. Relax your *arms and hands only*.
3. Now walk away from the wall, head up, buttocks in, shoulders straight. Look at yourself in the mirror. You should not look stiff. If you do, try it again. Walk around the room until you feel and look comfortable in this posture. Try it once a day, and think tall!

Another good exercise—one that will help keep your back straight—can be done many times during the day: stand or sit with straight back, and rotate your shoulders in a backward movement. Try to keep them erect with your head high at all times.

Your posture will improve with continued exercise, and, in time, good posture will become a natural part of you. Thus, you will look more attractive to your audience.

Diction

Closely related to your voice and poise is diction. You tell a story through language; therefore, you must be attuned to it. In telling stories, you have the privilege of sharing this phenomenon of language with children and of arousing their interest and delight in its rich fabric; its changing hues; its facets, depths, and varieties.

As a storyteller, you must have more than a rich and colorful vocabulary, although this is a necessary possession; you must be concerned with diction, which is the style and arrangement of words. The ability to use words with artistry and sensitivity comes naturally to the poet; it should and can be acquired by the storyteller. Ask yourself the following questions. Am I overworking certain adjectives at the expense of more descriptive words? Are my sentences too long or too short or lacking in variety? Do I tend to use too involved sentences in which the meaning gets lost? Am I faithful to the original story? Should I use more of the author's expressions and phrases? As you form your own answers, they will lead to an improvement of your diction and you will recreate a story for your audience with freshness and vigor.

Dialects

When should a storyteller use a dialect? This must be answered by each storyteller individually. A dialect may be intriguing and enchanting. Or it may be confusing, even offensive. You must attempt dialect with care, and use it only if the story requires it. It is far better to steer clear of dialect altogether than to risk botching it. Remember that storytelling is different from impersonation or acting. A storyteller tells a narrative in his own voice and manner and can only *suggest* through skillful use of tone and inflection the real sound of his characters' voices. If a whole story is written in dialect, you must consider carefully whether it is within your capabilities. Consider these illustrations.

If a story is set in Ireland and if the author's language is lilting and rich in Irish expressions and cadence and *if* you have the *ability* to capture the Irish flavor and inflection, then by all means use the Irish "dialect." Irish speech is melodic and adds much to the enjoyment of the story if the teller can carry it off. Even without the full rich speech, the storyteller can give a suggestion of the dialect. The first paragraph of Seumas MacManus's story "Jack and the King Who Was a Gentleman"[1] offers an example of the musical flow of the Irish speech.

> Well childre: wanst upon a time, when
> pigs was swine, there was a poor widdy
> woman lived all alone with her wan son
> Jack in a wee hut of a house, that on a
> dark night ye may aisily walk over it
> by mistake, not knowin' at all, at all,
> it was there, barrin', ye'd happen to
> strike yer toe again' it.

Much practice is required to capture the lilt of such phrases as "a wee hut of a house" or "not knowin' at all, at all, it was there"; but if the storyteller can capture the rhythm and the cadence, the storytelling is greatly enhanced. Tempo, inflection, and melody are key points to remember. Pronunciation, too, is different from American English with subtle differences in vowel sounds, dropped *g*'s, and trilled *r*'s. Harold Wentworth's *American Dialect Dictionary*, used extensively by actors, is recommended for storytellers who want to reproduce dialects accurately.

In Wanda Gág's story *Gone Is Gone*, I like to use a faint touch of German accent, but it is not necessary. I say, "Gone iss gone," and my inflections suggest the blustering, stocky Fritzl and his practical wife, Leisi. The *w*'s become slightly modified *v*'s with just a trace of an accent. I did not plan it this way; it just happened. I dearly love the story, and each time I told it to myself during the learning period, I became more and more identified with those comical young farm people, and the accent persisted. Was this right or wrong? All I can say is that it was right for me.

There is a grave danger in some uses of dialect. Racial and ethnic minorities have often been offended by dialect characterizations. Blacks, Latin Americans, Jews, Poles, and Italians have been particularly sensitive to certain derogatory stereotypes. It does not matter how farcical or amusing a story may be, the hurt can still occur. As a storyteller, you want every person in your audience to identify personally with the characters in your story, and no one enjoys being belittled or being identified with demeaning traits. Storytelling is a delicate and personal art. For narrow, professional reasons, as well as the broader, humanitarian considerations, you must avoid any use of a dialect that may be construed as a slur upon a racial or ethnic group.

The southern black dialect presents this problem in several stories of almost classical stature. For years, "Epaminondas and His Auntie," as written by Sara Cone Bryant, was a favorite story of mine as was "Little Black Sambo" by

34

Helen Bannerman. I was not aware that they offended some black people. But I have learned that they do. Incidentally, "Epaminondas," sans dialect, has been effectively retold by Eve Merriam. The illustrations by Trina Schart Hyman portray a well-meaning and delightful little boy without any identifying race or nationality. The story itself remains as good a story as it ever was, indicating that the story does not depend intrinsically on dialect or racial implications.

Once you have eliminated the possibility of offending your listeners, the best judge of the appropriateness of a dialect story is your audience. If the audience accepts your dialect and finds it natural and easy to follow, you may reap the benefits of its charm; if the audience is restless or unresponsive, your "dialect is showing" and probably needs practice or discontinuance. Storytelling with a dialect is a special skill. Experimentation in the early stages of telling and much practice as time goes on are required for the ease essential to its use.

Props and Gestures

Many people use gimmicks or gadgets for the story hour, and if they enjoy them, they need no further justification for their use. Personally, I prefer not to use them except in showing picture books. At times, props may be helpful in creating a proper atmosphere for a story hour, and at other times they may comfort the storyteller. They should not be deemed indispensable to storytelling.

The only prop I use is the book from which the story came. If I introduce a book before or after the story, some child may become interested and want to read the remaining stories in it. In fact, a good way to introduce the story hour is to show the children several books and say, "Now I'm going to tell you a story from this book," and hold it up for all to see. If you are going to share a picture-storybook, you should hold the book all through the story in such a way that the children can see and enjoy each picture.

As for gestures, use them if they are natural to you or if they emphasize an important part of the story and heighten the appreciation of the listeners. In telling the story "The Peddler and His Caps," you might want to put your hands over your head to show just how the little old peddler puts one cap on top of the other. Practicing in front of a mirror should help you determine whether your gestures add to or detract from the story. The story is the important thing, and it should stand on its own merit. If it is a good story and if you have learned it well, you will not need to rely on gestures.

Some storytellers use gimmicks at the beginning of a story hour to help the children get settled and to create an atmosphere conducive to listening. Some use a ritualistic ceremony such as lighting a candle and setting it on a nearby table or pedestal. Some play a musical recording in the background while the children find their places and get seated. In a park or playground, I have seen a child, acting as a storyteller's assistant and dressed in bright costume, walk around jingling a bell and telling children it is storytelling time. Any one of these devices is an effective way to begin a story hour; each storyteller must discover which is best for him.

I know a librarian who employs a flannel board not so much for her use in telling the story, but for the children's enjoyment after the story hour. She says the children like to retell the story themselves and manipulate the characters on the flannel board as they please—even changing some of the action. I strongly favor using any participation that the storyteller can elicit from his audience. A flannel board used in this way is great, although, strictly for myself, I prefer the story clear and uncluttered.

For small children, some variety during the story hour is usually a good idea. Some storytellers play a marching record and let the little children stretch by marching around the room. In such a situation, I have seen a storyteller put an elastic bracelet with bells attached on each child's wrist, so that, as he marched, he made bell music too. Another way to achieve a change of pace is with finger plays, described in Chapter 5.

Films and records play a definite and much needed role in the home, the classroom, and the school library. They are not, however, a substitute for a story hour with a real storyteller who can look into the eyes of eager listeners and adjust his or her telling of the story to the reactions of the audience. An inexperienced storyteller once sought to justify her use of the record for *A Story, a Story* by saying that the narrator told it so much better than she could. My advice to her was to listen to the recording herself and to study it so that she could improve her own telling. Storytellers should listen not only to themselves but to other storytellers, and recordings are a splendid means for such study. I believe that gimmicks, gadgets, records, and films are often used by people who feel their own telling ability is limited or inadequate. The solution is not a new gadget or a commercially made film or recording; rather, it is more study, more reading, more listening, and more practice.

Picture-Storybooks

As story hours are increasingly held for preschool children, storytellers are turning more and more to picture-storybooks. And the picture-storybooks available are many and truly wonderful. In picture-storybooks, the text is usually sparse whereas the pictures are most important. They reinforce the text and indeed almost tell the story themselves. This means that the storyteller must share the *pictures* with the children. This is hard to do unless the storyteller practically knows the story by heart. At least, you must know the story so well that a quick glance at the page reminds you of the text. Holding the book so that the children can see the pictures is a matter of practice. Try holding it at the bottom with one hand, and turn the pages with the other. Or you may prefer holding it at the top. Try changing hands, thereby letting children on each far side see the pictures too. Practicing with the book and in front of the mirror is the best way to master the technique of "telling" picture-storybooks. An excellent film, *The Pleasure Is Mutual*, with an accompanying booklet by Joanna Foster on picture-storybook programs has been published by the Westchester County Library System in New York (see page 121). I recommend them both to all storytellers who have preschoolers in their audience.

The Live Performance

Prepare as you may, the moment for performance arrives too soon, and you have no alternative but to smile and tell your stories. Many big eyes are looking at you; little ears want to hear your every word; you are one person talking directly to others. I have only a few words of offstage advice: (1) look directly at your audience, and make each child think you are talking to him personally; (2) keep your tempo lively and fairly quick—do not drag the story; (3) use your eyes and facial expression to help enliven the story; (4) *suggest*

different voices for certain characters, but beware of overdo-
ing this; do not attempt to be an impersonator; (5) on the
whole, keep the story conversational, simple, and direct; and
(6) do not disguise your own enjoyment of the story—tell it
as though you really love it and want to share it.

Interruptions

Be prepared for the unexpected during a story hour. Your
carefully rehearsed plan may be upset when you meet the
children face to face! Interruptions, especially from very
little children, are more the rule than the exception. They
may want to comment on the characters in the story or ask
questions about the pictures or tell you something that
happened on their way to the story hour. The storyteller
must accept such interruptions patiently and proceed with
the story when the children are ready for it. If the interruptions threaten to continue overlong or if they are all caused
by one child, the storyteller can say, "Now Mary, let's save
your questions until later and finish our story." If one child
brings a toy that appears to be a distraction, suggest putting
the toy on the table until after the story hour. If one child is
particularly wiggly, do not make an issue of it; just ignore
him or her and proceed with the story.

Testing With an Audience

As a storyteller, you cannot be sure about a story until you
have tested it on a real audience. The children know if the
story is too long, too involved, or too removed from their own
interests or experience; and you must be acutely sensitive to
their reactions. It is easy to sense the children's interest and

delight in a story, for it shows clearly in their eyes, their posture, their laughter, or their stillness as they listen. Their dislike or lack of interest is not so readily discerned, but you must learn to detect it too. Any signs of discomfiture should make you quicken your tempo, project your story with deeper expression, and perhaps skip over some details that, in the telling, bore the listeners.

On occasion, it may even be necessary to end a story abruptly. It is far better to bring a story to a quick close than to plow through it to the end if the children show signs of weariness or indifference. When such a situation occurs, skip as quickly as possible to the happy ending. If ending the story seems an impossible task, simply say, "Oh, children, I think this story isn't just what we want today. Let's save it for another time." And go immediately into another story—one that is short, humorous, and universally appealing. Do not worry about the children's reaction; they will probably be relieved, and so will you.

Sometimes after the first story an experienced storyteller finds it expedient to change the remainder of the program because of a feeling that there has been a miscalculation about the maturity and sophistication of the audience. Only an experienced storyteller can make on-the-spot changes with aplomb, but all storytellers must learn to abridge stories even during the telling if and when they sense that the audience is growing tired.

Be Your Own Critic

Perhaps the best advice for the storyteller is that one should become his or her own critic. Look at yourself, and listen to yourself objectively. Do you tend to slouch or let your stomach muscles sag? Do you speak carelessly with blurred words and slurred word endings? Do you say "Yeah" instead of "Yes"; "I'm gonna go" instead of "I am going"; "Ah'n't know" instead of "I don't know"? Do you talk without using your lips? Do you vary your inflection and pitch when occasion demands it, or do you use a monotonous inflection and an unvarying pitch? Do you speak too slowly or too rapidly? Do you have little mannerisms of speech such as "ya know," "like, for instance," "anyhow," "this boy" instead of "a boy"? Do you habitually start a sentence and leave it in midair while you go on to another? Unattractive mannerisms of speech can easily be overcome if you become aware of them. And an excellent way to become aware of one's speech patterns is to practice with a tape recorder.

A Successful Presentation

Spending time with a dictionary, a tape recorder, a mirror, and the *story* during weeks of preparation will assure you a successful presentation. In the final telling of the story, the technique or mechanics involved will operate unconsciously, and you will be able to give yourself wholeheartedly to the joy of the story and the delight of the children.

As each new story is selected, unfortunately, the same procedure must be followed and the same steps taken. One hopes that they will come more easily. The storyteller should be ever watchful and ever critical of his own style, image, voice, speech, and diction. Storytelling is indeed an art that requires study, practice, and vigilance, as does any art. It is also a source of great personal fulfillment and satisfaction.

NOTES FOR CHAPTER 3

1. Seumas MacManus, *Chimney Corners* (New York: Doubleday, 1899).

Chapter 4 READING AND SPEAKING POETRY

Poetry should be a part of every storyteller's background and repertoire. It cannot and should not be taught by the storyteller, but it can and should be shared.

The Poet's Language

Even though the fishmonger and the poet have language in common and each uses it to express his needs, his beliefs, and his dreams, in the poet's hands language is lifted out of the mundane marketplace and transformed.

Robert Frost said, "A poem is never a put-up job, so to speak. It begins as a lump in the throat, a sense of wrong, a homesickness, a love-sickness. It is never a thought to begin with. . . . It finds the thought, and the thought finds the words."[1] When we read a poem, we marvel at its spontaneity, its freshness, and naturalness. Like these lines by William Wordsworth,[2]

> My heart leaps up when I behold
> A rainbow in the sky:
> So was it when my life began;
> So is it now I am a man;
> So be it when I shall grow old,
>   Or let me die!
> The child is father of the Man;
> And I could wish my days to be
> Bound each to each by natural piety.

and these by Robert Browning,[3]

Grow old along with me;
The best is yet to be—
The last of life, for which
The first was made.

Poetry, like song, should be heard. And like good music, it must be heard again and again until the listener's ear becomes attuned to the rhythm, the meter, and the oral tapestry of language. Read poetry aloud to yourself. Let the magic lilt of it sing itself into your heart. Listen to its beat, its rhythm, its tone, and its cadences. Let the sound of it charm you; let the thought of it move you; let its imagery stir your imagination.

Children are close to poetry from infancy; they respond delightedly to rhythm, meter, and rhyme. Even a tiny baby enjoys having us say, "Pat-a-cake" as we clap his hands together. This natural delight in rhythmical language must be tenderly nurtured, treasured, and developed. Children love the sound of rhymed verse even when they do not always understand its meaning. And that is quite all right. Let us not analyze and dissect poetry for children. Archibald MacLeish's words, "A poem should not mean/But be!"[4] should be our rule. A poem cannot be forced on a child, but a child can be led to it. It lies waiting between the covers of a book.

Oral Interpretation of Poetry

Even more than storytelling, reading or speaking poetry aloud requires thoughtful study and much practice. Make tape recordings of your reading, and listen critically to them.

Listen to recordings of professional readers, and analyze their technique without attempting to imitate them.

It is not necessary to be dramatically sonorous; indeed, a straightforward, conversational voice and manner frequently achieve better understanding and greater delight. Even though you do not explain poetry to children, you, the storyteller, as part of your preparation, must be sure you know the meaning of each word, each line, and the relationship of each to the whole poem. Complete understanding is fundamental to clear and accurate interpretation.

Select a short poem with which to practice your technique.

THE DREAM KEEPER[5]
by Langston Hughes

Bring me all of your dreams,
You dreamers,
Bring me all of your
Heart melodies
That I may wrap them
In a blue cloud-cloth
Away from the too-rough fingers
Of the world.

An easy poem to understand, "The Dream Keeper" nevertheless contains pitfalls for the inexperienced reader. The poem does not rhyme, but it has decided rhythm. The punctuation indicates that the entire poem is one "sentence" or thought and that, therefore, the reader cannot end the thought by dropping his or her voice with finality until the last word is spoken. You must decide where it is convenient—and plausible—to pause for a breath without breaking the thought. All this, you must consider as you prepare to read the poem aloud. How disastrous it would be to drop your voice at the end of each line as some readers are wont to do.

In the next poem, one must guard against a singsong recitation because the rhyme and the rhythm tempt one to stress the measured beat; but, at the same time, the reader should suggest a lullaby tempo.

WYNKEN, BLYNKEN AND NOD[6]
by Eugene Field

Wynken, Blynken, and Nod one night
    Sailed off in a wooden shoe—
Sailed on a river of crystal light,
    Into a sea of dew.
"Where are you going, and what do you wish?"
    The old moon asked the three.
"We have come to fish for the herring fish
    That live in this beautiful sea;
    Nets of silver and gold have we!"
        Said Wynken,
        Blynken,
        And Nod.

The old moon laughed and sang a song,
    As they rocked in the wooden shoe,
And the wind that sped them all night long
    Ruffled the waves of dew.
The little stars were the herring fish
    That lived in that beautiful sea—
"Now cast your nets wherever you wish—
    Never afeard are we";

So cried the stars to the fishermen three:
  Wynken,
  Blynken,
  And Nod.

All night long their nets they threw
  To the stars in the twinkling foam—
Then down from the skies came the wooden shoe,
  Bringing the fishermen home;

'Twas all so pretty a sail, it seemed
  As if it could not be,
And some folks thought 'twas a dream they dreamed
  Of sailing that beautiful sea—
But I shall name you the fishermen three:
  Wynken,
  Blynken,
  And Nod.

Wynken and Blynken are two little eyes,
  And Nod is a little head,
And the wooden shoe that sailed the skies
  Is a wee one's trundle-bed.

So shut your eyes while your mother sings
  Of wonderful sights that be,
And you shall see the beautiful things
  As you rock in the misty sea,
  Where the old shoe rocked the fishermen three:
  Wynken,
  Blynken,
  And Nod.

As you study and practice reading poetry aloud, it is important to remember that you are an interpreter. You must make the ideas of the poem clear to your listeners; you must convey the spirit of the poem and bring to them the beauty of the poetic language through your own personality and voice quality. This calls for voice work again. All of the exercises and principles of voice improvement for storytelling can be used to improve your reading and speaking of poetry. With verse, there are fewer words, and you must make each word express just what the poet intended.

I offer a few simple guides for oral interpretation of poetry:

1. Know what thoughts and mood you want to convey.
2. Know ahead of time, by marking the page, where you can conveniently and effectively pause.
3. Know how to take a necessary breath imperceptibly during such a pause.
4. Know which words to stress and which words to soften.
5. Know what the proper tempo for the poem is and where you should vary the tempo.
6. Know how to keep your "voice up" until the thought demands a downward inflection signaling finality.

Never hesitate to *repeat* a short poem if the children like it. They will probably like it even more the second time. Occasionally, after a single reading of a poem such as "April Rain Song" (see page 49), you may ask the children how they feel about the rain. After a minute or two of comments and conversation, a second reading of the poem just seems natural and necessary. In speaking "A Misty Morning" (see page 49), I like to speed the tempo in the last few lines, beginning "He began to compliment . . ." And it *demands* a repetition, usually with the children joining in for the last two or three lines.

Selecting Poems for the Story Hour

As you begin your quest for suitable poems, choose simple, short poems. Be sure they speak to you. You must like them so much that you have a deep desire to share them with children. Like stories, poetry defies easy classification for particular ages, but experience with children and with poetry will guide you to successful selection. Select poems that have strong rhythm, some story content, and melodic language. They can be gay or quiet. In either case, your voice and your facial expression will help to impart the spirit of the poem. Nursery rhymes are among the best to start with for very young children. They present rhythm and rhyme, good story content, and a natural musical quality.

Here are a few examples that I have used successfully with young children. You will want to make your own choices.

Several from Mother Goose:

There was an old woman tossed up in a basket,
Seventeen times as high as the moon;
Where she was going I couldn't but ask it,
For in her hand she carried a broom.
Old woman, old woman, old woman, quoth I,
Where are you going to up so high?
To brush the cobwebs off the sky!
May I go with you? Aye, by-and-by.

Bye, baby bunting,
Daddy's gone a-hunting,
To get a little rabbit skin
To wrap the baby bunting in.

Rock-a-bye, baby, on the tree top,
When the wind blows the cradle will rock;

When the bough bends the cradle will fall,
Down will come baby, cradle and all.

One misty, moisty morning,
When cloudy was the weather,
I chanced to meet an old man
Clothed all in leather;
He began to compliment,
And I began to grin,
How do you do, and how do you do,
And how do you do again?

Jack Sprat could eat no fat.
His wife could eat no lean;
And so betwixt them both, my dears,
They licked the platter clean.

Georgie Porgie, pudding and pie,
Kissed the girls and made them cry;
When the boys came out to play,
Georgie Porgie ran away.

And introduce short, contemporary poems.

APRIL RAIN SONG[7]
by Langston Hughes

Let the rain kiss you.
Let the rain beat upon your head with silver liquid drops.
Let the rain sing you a lullaby.

The rain makes still pools on the sidewalk.
The rain makes running pools in the gutter.
The rain plays a little sleep-song on our roof at night—
And I love the rain.

SPRING RAIN[8]
by Marchette Chute

The storm came up so very quick
    It couldn't have been quicker.
I should have brought my hat along.
    I should have brought my slicker.

My hair is wet, my feet are wet,
    I couldn't be much wetter.
I fell into a river once.
    But this is even better.

TIRED TIM[9]
by Walter de la Mare

Poor tired Tim! It's sad for him.
He lags the long bright morning through,
Ever so tired of nothing to do;
He moons and mopes the livelong day,
Nothing to think about, nothing to say;
Up to bed with his candle to creep,
Too tired to yawn, too tired to sleep;
Poor tired Tim! It's sad for him.

HALLOWE'EN[10]
by Harry Behn

Tonight is the night
When dead leaves fly
Like witches on switches
Across the sky,
When elf and sprite
Flit through the night
On a moony sheen.

Tonight is the night
When leaves make a sound
Like a gnome in his home
Under the ground,
When spooks and trolls
Creep out of holes
Mossy and green.

Tonight is the night
When pumpkins stare
Through sheaves and leaves
Everywhere.
When ghoul and ghost
And goblin host
Dance 'round the queen.

It's Hallowe'en!

Just as a very short story is useful to round out a story hour, so a poem can frequently be slipped into a program to add variety, change the pace, or create a mood. For example, after you have successfully shared McCloskey's picture book *Make Way for Ducklings*, why not read this poem?

REGENT'S PARK[11]
by Rose Fyleman

What makes the ducks in the pond, I wonder, go
Suddenly under?

Down they go in the neatest way;
You'd be surprised at the time they stay,
You stand on the bank and you wait and stare,
Trying to think what they do down there;
And, just as you're feeling anxious, then

Suddenly up they come again,
Ever so far from where you guessed,
Dry and tidy and self-possessed.

What is it makes the ducks, I wonder, go
Suddenly under?

After hearing the poem, the children may want to look at the ducks in McCloskey's book again.

After you have shared *Gilberto and the Wind* by Marie Hall Ets, it would be lovely to read this wind poem.

WIND ON THE HILL[12]
by A. A. Milne

No one can tell me,
Nobody knows,
Where the wind comes from,
Where the wind goes.

It's flying from somewhere
As fast as it can,
I couldn't keep up with it,
Not if I ran.

But if I stopped holding
The string of my kite,
It would blow with the wind
For a day and a night.

And then when I found it,
Wherever it blew,
I should know that the wind
Had been going there too.

> So then I could tell them
> Where the wind goes . . .
> But where the wind comes from
> *Nobody* knows.

You may find it worthwhile to collect a whole group of poems on different subjects to use with appropriate stories or picture books.

A helpful source for locating poems on a particular theme or subject is the *Subject Guide to Poetry for Children and Young People*, published by the American Library Association.

As you search for suitable poetry, do not overlook the Japanese haiku. These short, seventeen-syllable verses hold great fascination for young people. And because haiku does not rhyme, children often find it fun to compose their own. Ezra Jack Keats, author and illustrator of many children's books, has beautifully illustrated a book of haiku, edited by Richard Lewis, called *In a Spring Garden*. Ann Atwood's book *Haiku; the Mood of Earth* is an enriching experience for children and adults that combines her own haiku with her own photographs. Harry Behn's *Cricket Songs; Japanese Haiku* is still another enchanting collection to share with children.

Haiku affords the storyteller one more way to inspire the imagination of his or her audience. In addition to enjoying the verses, children are impressed by the necessary discipline of the poet as he or she adheres to the physical limitation of the haiku form.

A few examples of haiku follow:

> Two doves in a wood
>   Coo softy to each other,
> Celebrating spring.[13]

The brown thrasher sings
    And dares me to be busy.
I stop and listen.[14]

A giant firefly:
    that way, this way, that way, this—
    and it passes by.[15]

The storyteller must judge when and how lengthy an introduction of a poem should be given. Avoid labeling poetry. Do not formalize it. Poetry should just happen. After the first few times, the children will come to expect a poem or two at every story hour. They may even want to write some poems of their own, and if this happens, you can be sure your own reading has been successful.

Children are naturally creative and imaginative; and, given encouragement, they will frequently reveal their emotions and innermost thoughts with astonishing sensitivity, awareness, and beauty. As evidence of children's ability to express themselves poetically and poignantly, read these short selections:

MOUNTAINS[16]
by Sakai Akiko, age 7

Mountains
have nerves,
The roots of the trees
are the nerves of the mountains.
Mountains
have ears.
They copy what man says.
Everybody calls it
echoes.

RAIN[17]
by Leila Heron, age 8

I love rain
On a summer's day
When I have just been swimming
And the leaves rustle and the winds blow
And my mother calls
And says to get out of the water,
And we run home.
No animal seems to care
If it rains or snows
Or the winds blow
Oh I wonder why.

THE CITY[18]
by Juanita Bryant

The city is full of people
pushing and rushing for the check
The city is kids playing in the park
telling their mothers the hell with them.

It's full of hate and war
with people never knowing who to turn to for help.
It's a prison with people fighting for freedom
Black white.
The city's full of them.

THE THOUGHTS OF A CHILD[19]
by Denise Embry

I am a child.
But still I think,
I feel, I see,

I hear, I wonder.
Why do they hate us so?
I see their sneers and jeers.
I hear them laugh and call us awful names.

Some of us are ashamed of being Black.
But I know this
I'm not ashamed of being Black
I'm proud; I will stand tall.
They *cannot* make me fall.

TALKING[20]
by Michael Goode, age 12

Some people talk in the hall
Some people talk in a drawl
Some people talk, talk, talk, talk
And never say anything at all.

LIFE[21]
by Paul Goggins, age 13

Life can be good,
Life can be bad;
Life is mostly cheerful,
But sometimes sad.

Life can be dreams,
Life can be thoughts;
Life can mean a person,
Sitting in court.

Life can be *dirty,*
Life can even be painful;
But life is what you make it,
So try to make it beautiful.

THE FIRE HYDRANT[22]
by Ricky Preiskel, age 10

It's like a strange plant bursting with its juice.
Like a city's waterfall. I wouldn't be surprised
if a whale came out today.

Even if the children are not inspired to write their own
verse, they may want to read or speak a poem that has
meaning for them. This is fine and should be encouraged.
One of the most effective means of such encouragement is
to introduce children to choral speaking.

Choral Speaking

Choral speaking can be as simple as three children speaking "Baa, baa, blacksheep" together or as sophisticated as a
dramatic rendition of a Greek chorus in a large theater.
Speaking in unison is an old art that can be easily and
profitably adapted to the story hour. It is similar to a glee club
or singing choir except that it is a choir of speaking voices
without musical accompaniment.

For the story hour, the chief virtue of choral speaking is
that it requires audience participation, an important factor
in a successful program. It is also an effective way of helping
children experience directly the rhythm of the poetic form.
As a group activity, choral speaking shows children how
they can—indeed must—work as a team to speak in unison.
Incidentally, it gives the shy child a chance to speak while
remaining comparatively anonymous. Clear enunciation
and good speech habits are unconscious by-products of the
activity as the children learn that their voices are musical
instruments capable of making a diversity of sounds
through pitch, resonance, and careful use of lips, tongue,

and teeth. Finally, choral speaking is a pleasant and easy way to memorize poetry.

For very small children who cannot read, there can be no passing out of printed selections. All learning must be oral and heard, and consequently all selections must be very short. Therefore, the storyteller introduces the verse and invites the children to say it with him or her. Mother Goose comes to the fore once again. A good short verse to try in the beginning is

> Hickory, dickory, dock,
> The mouse ran up the clock.
> The clock struck one,
> The mouse ran down,
> Hickory, dickory, dock.

To make it a little more of a game, the children may speak the first two lines and the last line in chorus and the word *one!* while the storyteller says the rest.

Another short verse, which can be done with pairs of children clapping each other's hands, is

> Pease porridge hot,
> Pease porridge cold,
> Pease porridge in the pot,
> Nine days old.
> Some like it hot,
> Some like it cold,
> Some like it in the pot,
> Nine days old.

With the next verse, the children need only say "Poor thing," while the storyteller says the rest.

The north wind doth blow,
And we shall have snow,
And what will poor robin do then?
Poor thing.

He'll sit in the barn,
And keep himself warm,
And hide his head under his wing.
Poor thing.

The next has strong rhythm and offers good lip and tongue exercises for the sounds of *b, t, d,* and *m.*

Rub-a dub-dub.
Three men in a tub,
And who do you think they be?
The butcher, the baker,
The candlestick maker,
Turn 'em out knaves all three!

For older children, "The Grand Old Duke of York" is an exciting rhyme. The voices should get louder and then taper off; the speaking should stress the strong, martial beat.

The grand Old Duke of York
He had ten thousand men,
He marched them up a very high hill
and he marched them down again.
And when he was up he was up
and when he was down he was down
And when he was only halfway up
He was neither up nor down.

Sometimes just two lines of a longer poem are sufficient to say in unison. The following lines from "The Bells of London" (author unknown) are excellent as an exercise for the choir. Be sure they make the vowels round and full and almost sing the resonant consonants: *ng, ll,* "L*on* d*on*" "t*ow*n."

THE BELLS OF LONDON[23]
(author unknown)

Gay go up, and gay go down,
To ring the bells of London town.

In the next poem, the children say the first two lines and the last two lines while the storyteller speaks those in between. The children may want to do some real thumping and bumping.

THE GOBLIN[24]
by Rose Fyleman

A goblin lives in *our* house, in *our* house, in *our*
    house,
A goblin lives in *our* house all the year round.
He bumps
And he jumps
And he thumps
And he stumps
He knocks
And he rocks
And he rattles at the locks.
A goblin lives in *our* house, in *our* house, in *our*
    house,
A goblin lives in *our* house all the year round.

If the choral speaking continues in your story hour and shows signs of becoming an activity of greater interest and participation, you may want to group the voices or at least have boys speak certain lines, girls speak others, and, perhaps, a solo voice for a particular line or word. If the activity reaches this stage, as it well might in a classroom or scout group, the leader should distribute copies of the poem, classify the voices, and assign certain lines to the various members of the group. A word of caution: the leader should lead the group without dictating. Imitation is not the goal. Understanding, interpretation, and appreciation of poetry are the real objectives. To achieve these, the leader must listen to the children, respect their ideas and suggestions, and encourage them to express their opinions as to the meaning and mood of the poetry.

For anyone who has had no experience in listening or participating in choral speaking, let me point out that the leader's role is precisely the same as that of the leader of a glee club or chorus. The leader keeps time, indicates the crescendo and diminuendo moods, signals the solo voice and the groups assigned to certain lines, and *directs* the choir. The informality of an impromptu story hour choir reduces the director's autonomy to a fun and games mood. Otherwise, there is no difference.

Older boys and girls sometimes resist the appeal of poetry. With a little encouragement, however, their appreciation will spring to life and go forward unaided and free. Choral speaking does much to overcome shyness or self-consciousness in these "growing-up" children.

Edward Lear's and Lewis Carroll's nonsense poems are great fun for boys and girls. "The Owl and the Pussy Cat" and "The Jabberwocky" are particularly good for choral groups. If more serious poems appeal to them, there are many to choose from.

Do You Fear the Wind[25]
by Hamlin Garland

Do you fear the force of the wind,
The slash of the rain?
Go face them and fight them,
Be savage again.
Go hungry and cold like the wolf,
Go wade like the crane:
The palms of your hands will thicken,
The skin of your cheeks will tan,
You'll grow ragged, and weary and swarthy,
But you'll walk like a man!

Young people also enjoy strong, rhythmic ballads and marching songs such as "Sea Fever" by John Masefield or "The Flag Goes By" by Henry Holcomb Bennett. After some practice, they might speak this touching, quiet poem.

The Four Little Foxes[26]
by Lew Sarett

Speak gently, Spring, and make no sudden
    sound;
For in my windy valley, yesterday I found
New-born foxes squirming on the ground—
    Speak gently.

Walk softly, March, forbear the bitter blow;
Her feet within a trap, her blood upon the
    snow,
The four little foxes saw their Mother go—
    Walk softly.

Go lightly, Spring, oh, give them no alarm;
When I covered them with boughs to shelter
    them from harm,
The thin blue foxes suckled at my arm—
    Go lightly.

Step softly, March, with your rampant hurri-
    cane;
Nuzzling one another, and whimpering with
    pain,
The new little foxes are shivering in the rain—
    Step softly.

Poetry for Growing Up

Many poems written for adults may also be understood and loved by children. The obstacles to a child's comprehension of such poems lies not so much in imaginative expression but in the concept or subject matter. There is much overlapping and intertwining here, and we, as storytellers, must be able to select from the full range of excellent poetry, poems that will appeal to young, inexperienced listeners. To make this selection, we must ourselves read widely and continuously.

In the following selections, some poems are within the grasp of children and others are not. All, however, are meet for the storyteller's own background reading.

Consider the simple mood song of this first poem.

THE NIGHT WILL NEVER STAY[27]
by Eleanor Farjeon

The night will never stay,
The night will still go by,

> Though with a million stars
> You pin it to the sky,
> Though you bind it with the blowing wind
> And buckle it with the moon,
> The night will slip away
> Like sorrow or a tune.

Any youngster can capture its feeling and go on with his imagination as far as he is able.

Try Robert Frost's "A Time to Talk."

A TIME TO TALK[28]
by Robert Frost

> When a friend calls to me from the road
> And slows his horse to a meaning walk,
> I don't stand still and look around
> On all the hills I haven't hoed,
> And shout from where I am, 'What is it?'
>
> No, not as there is a time to talk.
> I thrust my hoe in the mellow ground,
> Blade-end up and five feet tall,
> And plod: I go up to the stone wall
> For a friendly visit.

A child will understand how good it is for friends to talk to each other, and it may lead him to consider the fellowship of man.

Another of Frost's simple verses may require more maturity.

FIRE AND ICE[29]
by Robert Frost

> Some say the world will end in fire,
> Some say in ice.

From what I've tasted of desire
I hold with those who favor fire.
But if it had to perish twice,
I think I know enough of hate
To say that for destruction ice
Is also great
And would suffice.

The next three poems find welcome listeners in almost any age group.

Fog[30]
by Carl Sandburg

The fog comes
on little cat feet.

It sits looking
over harbor and city
on silent haunches
and then moves on.

A Bird[31]
by Emily Dickinson

A bird came down the walk,
He did not know I saw;
He bit an angleworm in halves
And ate the fellow, raw.

And then he drank a dew
From a convenient grass,
And then hopped sidewise to the wall
To let a beetle pass.

. . . .

SOME ONE[32]
by Walter de la Mare

Some one came knocking
    At my wee, small door;
Some one came knocking,
    I'm sure—sure—sure;
I listened, I opened,
    I looked to left and right,
But nought there was a-stirring
    In the still dark night;
Only the busy beetle
    Tap-tapping in the wall,
Only from the forest
    The screech-owl's call,
Only the cricket whistling
    While the dewdrops fall,
So I know not who came knocking,
    At all, at all, at all.

The poetic message of Gabriela Mistral entitled "For Children" is not literally "for children," but rather for children who have grown to maturity.

FOR CHILDREN[33]
by Gabriela Mistral

Many years from now, when I am a little mound of silent dust, play with me, with the earth of my heart and my bones. Should a mason gather me up, he would make me into a brick, and I would be stuck forever in a wall, and I hate quiet corners . . . If they put me into the wall of a prison, I would blush with shame at hearing a man sob. Or if I became the wall of a school, I would suffer from not being able to sing with you in the mornings.

I had rather be dust that you play with on the country roads. Pound me, because I have been yours. Scatter me, as I did you. Stomp me because I never gave you truth entire and beauty whole. O, I mean, sing and run above me that I might kiss your precious footprints.

Say a pretty verse when you have me in your hands, and I will run with pleasure through your fingers. Uplifted at the sight of you, in your eyes I will look for the curly heads of those I taught.

And when you have made of me some sort of statue, shatter it each time, as each time before children shattered me in tenderness and sorrow.

Lastly consider the beauty and the challenge of Theodore Roethke's "The Waking."

THE WAKING[34]
by Theodore Roethke

I wake to sleep, and take my waking slow.
I feel my fate in what I cannot fear.
I learn by going where I have to go.

We think by feeling. What is there to know?
I hear my being dance from ear to ear.
I wake to sleep, and take my waking slow.

Of those so close beside me, which are you?
God bless the Ground! I shall walk softly there,
And learn by going where I have to go.

Light takes the Tree; but who can tell us how?
The lowly worm climbs up a winding stair;
I wake to sleep, and take my waking slow.

Great Nature has another thing to do
To you and me; so take the lively air,
And, lovely, learn by going where to go.

This shaking keeps me steady. I should know.
What falls away is always. And is near.
I wake to sleep, and take my waking slow.
I learn by going where I have to go.

Containing no phrase that a child cannot understand, "The Waking" evokes a mystery and philosophy of life that older children can begin to comprehend.

Poetry reading, interspersed in a program of storytelling, is sparkling entertainment. It can cast a spell that will hold you and your listeners together.

NOTES FOR CHAPTER 4

1. Robert Frost, *The Letters of Robert Frost to Louis Untermeyer* (New York: Holt, Rinehart and Winston, 1963). Letter dated January 1, 1916.
2. William Wordsworth, *The Complete Poetical Works of William Wordsworth* (London: Macmillan, 1898).
3. Robert Browning, "Rabbi Ben Ezra," in *The Complete Poetic and Dramatic Works of Robert Browning* (Boston: Houghton Mifflin, 1895).
4. Archibald MacLeish, "Ars Poetica," in *Collected Poems 1917–1952* (Boston: Houghton Mifflin, 1952).
5. Langston Hughes, *Don't You Turn Back: Poems by Langston Hughes* (New York: Alfred A. Knopf, 1969).
6. Eugene Field, *Poems of Childhood* (New York: Charles Scribner's Sons, 1974).
7. Langston Hughes, op. cit.
8. Marchette Chute, *Around and About* (New York: Dutton, 1957).

9. Walter de la Mare, *Complete Poems of Walter de la Mare* (New York: Alfred A. Knopf, 1970).
10. Harry Behn, *The Little Hill; Poems and Pictures* (New York: Harcourt, Brace and World, 1949).
11. Rose Fyleman, *Gay Go Up* (Garden City, N.Y.: Doubleday, 1929).
12. A. A. Milne, *Now We Are Six* (New York: Dutton, 1927).
13. Rebecca Caudill, *Come Along!* (New York: Holt, Rinehart and Winston, 1969).
14. Ibid.
15. Harold G. Henderson, *An Introduction to Haiku* (Garden City, N.Y.: Doubleday, 1958).
16. Richard Lewis, ed., *There Are Two Lives; Poems by Children of Japan,* translated by Haruna Kimura (New York: Simon & Schuster, 1970).
17. Richard Lewis, ed., *Miracles; Poems by Children of the English-Speaking World* (New York: Simon & Schuster, 1966).
18. Nancy Larrick, comp., *I Heard a Scream in the Street; Poems by Young People in the City* (Philadelphia: J.B. Lippincott, 1970).
19. Ibid.
20. June Jordan and Terri Bush, comps., *The Voice of the Children* (New York: Holt, Rinehart and Winston, 1970).
21. Ibid.
22. Richard Lewis, ed., *Journeys; Prose by Children of the English-Speaking World* (New York: Simon & Schuster, 1969).
23. Burton Egbert Stevenson, *The Home Book of Verse . . .* (New York: Henry Holt, 1953).
24. Rose Fyleman, *Picture Rhymes from Foreign Lands* (Philadelphia: J.B. Lippincott, 1942).
25. Burton Egbert Stevenson, op. cit.
26. Lew Sarett, *Covenant with Earth; a Selection from the Poetry of Lew Sarett,* edited by Alma Sarett (Gainesville, Florida: University of Florida Press, 1956).
27. Eleanor Farjeon, *Poems for Children* (Philadelphia: J.B. Lippincott, 1926).
28. Robert Frost, *The Poetry of Robert Frost,* edited by Edward Connery Latham (New York: Holt, Rinehart and Winston, 1969).
29. Ibid.
30. Carl Sandburg, *Early Moon,* illustrated by James Daugherty (New York: Harcourt, Brace, 1930).
31. Emily Dickinson, *Poems of Emily Dickinson,* selected by Helen Plotz (New York: Thomas Y. Crowell, 1964).
32. Walter de la Mare, op. cit.
33. Gabriela Mistral, *Selected Poems of Gabriela Mistral,* translated by Langston Hughes (Bloomington: Indiana University Press, 1957).
34. Theodore Roethke, *The Collected Poems of Theodore Roethke* (New York: Doubleday, 1966).

Chapter 5   CREATIVE DRAMATICS

"**I**'LL BE the mother and you be my little girl," is an often-heard exclamation in the nursery school or on the playground as children fall easily and unself-consciously into the world of make-believe. Here, they dramatize their inhibitions, their hurts, their dreams, and their desires through creative and imaginative play. Acting out stories and verses is a natural extension of children's simple, homely, dramatic activity.

Depending on the storyteller's talent, insight, and ambition and on the children's state of mind and mood, the story hour can, on occasion, also become an acting-out place. Given the right combination of circumstances and motivation, it can assume an entirely new and altogether delightful dimension, which includes not only choral speaking but creative dramatics as well.

Finger Plays

When very small children come to a story hour for the first time and do not know what to expect, you can introduce one or two finger plays as a method of getting acquainted. Greet the children, and help them get comfortably seated on the floor. If you are lucky, a child will make a comment that can be used to lead off a brief, informal conversation with the group. You might then lift up the index finger of your right hand and say, "Let's pretend this is Billy, shall we?" And from that you can proceed to the first finger play.

Billy came outside his house to play.
He looked up the street and down the street.
(Finger bends to right, then left.)
He didn't see anyone to play with
So he went back into the house.
(His finger disappears.)

Now raise the index finger of the left hand and repeat,
except that this time it is Betty who looks for someone to play
with.

Next day, they both come out at the same time.
(Raise index finger of each hand.)
They look up the street and don't see anyone.
Then they look down the street and they see each other!
They are very happy (fingers bob up and down), and they
play together. Finally, it's time to go in. Billy goes
to his house and Betty goes to hers.
(Separate hands and return to original position.)
They both say, "Good-bye. I'll see you tomorrow!"
And Billy goes into his house and
Betty goes into her house.
(Return both fingers to respective fists.)
The children watch as Betty and Billy disappear and reappear. Then, quite casually and naturally, you invite the children to play the game with you. Some will, and a few may not. But they will all watch very intently. And so their attention is caught and the storytelling can begin. After one, or at the most, two stories, the children will need a moment of stretching and relaxation. This time you might have them stand up and stretch their arms high and round to make the sun and then let their fingers and arms come down in little

rain drops. When the children are seated again, introduce them to the finger play of Eensey Weensy Spider.

. EENSY, WEENSY SPIDER
(author unknown)

The eensy, weensy spider
    (Extend and curve fingers of the right hand.)
Climbed up the water spout.
    (Fingers climb, spider fashion, up the left arm.)
Down came the rain
    (Both arms and hands make downward motion
    for the rain.)
And washed the spider out.

Out came the sun
    (Form a big circle with arms over head.)
And dried up all the rain.
So eensy, weensy spider
    (Make spider with curled fingers.)
Climbed up the spout again.
    (Repeat climbing up left arm with right fingers.)

After such physical activity and a little talking, the children can settle back and listen quietly to another story.

The next time these same children attend a story hour, they will know what to expect. You must decide if the "ice breaker" is necessary at the beginning and just when, during the story hour, a finger-play diversion is appropriate. You may repeat the ones the children did the first time and add a new one. The children will learn the words of the finger plays as they manipulate their fingers. And this is the beginning of unself-conscious acting-out.

THE BIG CLOCK
(author unknown)

Slowly ticks the big clock;
(Make a big, round clock with both hands in front.)

Tick-tock, tick-tock!
(Clap hands four times to slow rhythm.)

But Cuckoo clock ticks double quick;
(Make a smaller clock with both hands.)

Tick-a-tock-a, tick-a-tock-a,
Tick-a-tock-a, tick!
(Hold hands in front. Open and close them
rapidly to represent the Cuckoo.)

To the tune of the song "Frère Jacques," the next finger
play can be sung, first by you and then with you by all the
children.

Where is Thumbkin? Where is Thumbkin?
(Make fists.)
Here he is. Here he is.
(Hold up first one thumb and then the other.)
How are you today, sir?
(Left thumb nods.)
Very well, I thank you.
(Right thumb nods.)
Run away. (Left wrist retreats
behind child.)
Run away. (Right wrist retreats.)

(The gestures are the same for the remainder of the song;
   use the appropriate finger for each verse.)

Where is Pointer? Where is Pointer?
Here he is. Here he is.
How are you today, sir?
Very well, I thank you.
Run away. Run away.

Where is Middleman? Where is Middleman? And so on.

Where is Ring Finger? Where is Ring Finger? And so on.

Where is Pinky? Where is Pinky? And so on.

Where is Everybody? Where is Everybody? And so on.

FIVE LITTLE SAUSAGES
(author unknown)

Five little sausages
Frying in a pan
   (Hold up five fingers.)
All of a sudden
One sausage went bam!
   (Clap hands.)

Four little sausages
Frying in a pan
   (Hold up four fingers.)
And so on until all sausages are gone; then—

No little sausages
Frying in a pan
   (Look mournful.)
All of a sudden
The *pan* went bam! (A loud clap.)

Body Play

Finger plays can be extended to body play, in which there is a greater movement and a bit of jostling. For instance, during the "break" in the story hour, children can sit on the floor in pairs, holding hands and facing each other with legs stretched out. They speak the following Mother Goose rhyme in unison with a back and forth movement:

> Jack and Jill went up the hill,
> To fetch a pail of water;
> Jack fell down, and broke his crown,
> And Jill came tumbling after.

This can be repeated in double-quick time and usually ends in laughter and a good tumble onto the floor. Another body play verse that can be acted out with imaginative play is

THE WHIRL AND TWIRL
(author unknown)

> Like a leaf or a feather,
> In the windy, windy weather;
> We will all whirl around
> And twirl all around
> And all sink down together.

Following this type of activity, quietly speak (or sing) a soothing lullaby. The children may hold an imaginary baby in their arms and rock rhythmically as they listen to the poem.

SWEET AND LOW[1]
by Alfred, Lord Tennyson

Sweet and low, sweet and low,
    Wind of the western sea,
Low, low, breathe and blow,
    Wind of the western sea!
Over the rolling waters go,
Come from the dying moon, and blow,
    Blow him again to me;
While my little one, while my pretty one,
    sleeps.

Sleep and rest, sleep and rest,
    Father will come to thee soon;
Rest, rest on mother's breast,
    Father will come to thee soon;
Father will come to his babe in the nest,
Silver sails all out of the west
    Under the silver moon;
Sleep my little one, sleep, my pretty one,
    Sleep.

Acting Out Verse

Turning once more to Mother Goose, we find an abundance of good, dramatic material to use with very young children. A very actable verse is "Little Miss Muffet." Although there are only two characters, Miss Muffet and the Spider, the verse is so short that it can be repeated several times with a new cast each time. As an alternative, the verse can be spoken by the group while little Miss Muffet and the villainous spider play their parts in pantomime. Children love it, and most of them want to be the spider!

Little Miss Muffet
Sat on a tuffet
Eating her curds and whey;
There came a big spider,
Who sat down beside her
And frightened Miss Muffet away.

Another verse drama, "Little Jack Horner," is easily done with one child at a time playing Jack in pantomime while the children speak the verse in unison. When they reach the last line, they stop after "and said—" and Jack says in a loud, clear voice, "What a big boy am I!" Of course, many children may have a turn to be Jack. There might even be four Jacks simultaneously, each in a different corner of the "stage."

Little Jack Horner
Sat in a corner
Eating a Christmas pie;
He put in his thumb,
And pulled out a plum,
And said, "What a big boy am I!"

The next verses are good for encouraging children to jump nimbly, lightly, and accurately. Because these rhymes are frequently used for jumping rope, two children can *pretend* to twirl a rope while a third does the jumping. This calls for pretty good coordination and is most successfully done by eight- and nine-year-olds; but the verse *minus* the rope-twirling can be done with very small children.

Jack be nimble,
Jack be quick,
Jack jump over
The candlestick.

Jump it lively,
Jump it quick,
But don't knock over
The candlestick.

A very humorous pantomime can be worked out by imaginative youngsters with:

DOCTOR FOSTER

Doctor Foster went to Gloucester
In a shower of rain;
He stepped in a puddle,
Right up to his middle,
And never went there again.

A great favorite, but one that is better for older children because of its length, is "The Three Little Kittens." This calls for a cast of four—the mother cat and the three little kittens. The rest of the children speak the narrative verses in unison.

GROUP:
Three little kittens they lost their mittens,
    And they began to cry,

KITTENS:
Oh, mother dear, we sadly fear
    That we have lost our mittens.

MOTHER:
What! Lost your mittens, you naughty kittens!
    Then you shall have no pie.

KITTENS:
Mee-ow, mee-ow, mee-ow.

MOTHER:
No, you shall have no pie.

GROUP:
The three little kittens they found their mittens,
    And they began to cry,

KITTENS:
Oh, Mother dear, see here, see here,
    For we have found our mittens.

MOTHER:
Put on your mittens, you silly kittens,
    And you shall have some pie.

KITTENS:
Purr-r, purr-r, purr-r,
Oh, let us have some pie.

GROUP:
The three little kittens put on their mittens,
    And soon ate up the pie;

KITTENS:
Oh, mother dear, we greatly fear
    That we have soiled our mittens.

MOTHER:
What! Soiled your mittens, you naughty kittens!

GROUP:
Then they began to sigh

KITTENS:
Mee-ow, mee-ow, mee-ow,

GROUP:
Then they began to sigh.

GROUP:
The three little kittens they washed their mittens,
    And hung them out to dry;

KITTENS:
Oh, Mother dear, do you not hear
    That we have washed our mittens?

MOTHER:
What! washed your mittens, then you're good
    kittens.

KITTENS:
Mee-ow, mee-ow, mee-ow,
We smell a rat close by.

Pantomime

Pantomime is an enriching experience and is frequently easier for children than "saying lines" in a formal play. In the following poem, you speak the words while the children slish and slosh around in imaginary galoshes. The word *galoshes* may be new to the children because the vogue of "boots" has become common usage, but *galoshes* is such a good mouthful of a word that children should be introduced to it. After the poem, they might continue to move around in small groups pretending there is one big puddle to cross. The pantomime and even improvised dialogue can be encouraged between repeated readings of the poem.

GALOSHES[2]
by Rhoda Bacmeister

Susie's galoshes
Make splishes and sploshes
And slooshes and sloshes,
As Susie steps slowly
Along in the slush.

They stamp and they tramp
On the ice and concrete,
They get stuck in the muck and the mud;
But Susie likes much best to hear

The slippery slush
As it slooshes and sloshes,
And splishes and sploshes,
All round her galoshes!

Incidentally, the episode of Ramona and her new, red boots
in Beverly Cleary's *Ramona, the Pest* can be read or told to
the children before or after introducing the galoshes poem.

Harry Behn's "The Kite" offers boys and girls a delightful
theme for creativity. They can speak the poem in unison and
then have two or three boys fly their kites in pantomime.

THE KITE[3]
by Harry Behn

How bright on the blue
Is a kite when it's new!

With a dive and a dip
It snaps its tail

Then soars like a ship
With only a sail

As over tides
Of wind it rides,

Climbs to the crest
Of a gust and pulls,

Then seems to rest
As wind falls.

When string goes slack
You wind it back

And run until
A new breeze blows

And its wings fill
And up it goes!

How bright on the blue
Is a kite when it's new!

But a raggeder thing
You never will see

When it flaps on a string
In the top of a tree.

If their interest is high, the children can "fly" their kites as they improvise dialogue based on the poem; for example, "See my bright blue kite! It's new! Watch it dive and dip and snap its tail," and so forth.

Pantomime without supporting words fascinates bigger children—eight years old and over. If the group is not too large, give each child a turn to do one pantomime while the rest of the children try to figure out what he is doing.

Before you ask the children to do this, you should do one or two pantomimes yourself to show them how it is done. This means that you must practice beforehand. These suggestions should help you acquire the skill:

1. Know ahead of time exactly what you want to convey.
2. Begin with a very simple activity.
3. Practice with actual objects first. If you are supposed to be holding a cup and saucer in your hand, practice by actually holding a cup and saucer, and observe precisely how you do it. If you are going to thread a needle, actually thread the needle, and observe each detail of the operation. Then practice without the cup and saucer or the needle and thread. Always practice in front of a mirror to see if you are convincing to yourself.
4. If you plan to eat or drink something in pantomime, decide ahead of time exactly what the food or drink is. You should know if it is hard or soft, chewy or mushy, bitter or sweet, hot or cold, pleasant or unpleasant. If you know these things, your audience will successfully guess your pantomime.
5. Avoid whispering or mouthing words, and *never* talk. Your facial expression, your body, head, eyes, and hands must express the mood, the action, and the kind of person you are creating.
6. Beware of being too ambitious in the beginning. A story with a great deal of action and change of scene is very difficult to execute in pantomime. Begin with simple actions and moods, and proceed to more complex situations after your first efforts have proved successful.

After you have aroused the children's interest with your own pantomimic exercises, let them try it. If they can't think of simple actions to portray, give them these or similar suggestions:

1. Walk like an old, old man who has a backache.
2. Put on your boots that are a little too tight.
3. Wash and dry your hands.
4. Pour milk into a glass, and drink a little.
5. Try to get a lid off a box that is very tight.
6. Step carefully over a puddle of water while wearing your best shoes.
7. Walk on the sidewalk without stepping on a crack.
8. Play hopscotch, and miss after the second jump.
9. Chew bubble gum, and create a bubble.
10. Blow up a balloon so big that it pops.

After children have done simple pantomimes, they can progress to group activities. This requires group planning and practice and will probably lead to the creation of simple plots. The group must agree on the characters, the problem to be presented, and the effect to be achieved. Warn them to leave nothing to chance. Work out each element of the action.

Here are some simple group pantomimes to suggest:

1. Two boys are playing with a ball, tossing it back and forth to each other. A third boy arrives and wants to join the game. At first, the two boys refuse, but soon they let him join them. He throws the ball so high that it goes over a high wall. The two boys are furious and go off to find the ball, and the third boy leaves dejected.
2. Two girls are jumping rope, each with her own rope. A third girl arrives, but has no rope. They decide to have two girls hold one rope at each end while the third one

takes a turn jumping. Each one gets a turn to jump until she misses. Then it is her turn to hold one end of the rope.
3. Four children—two boys and two girls—get into position to practice a folk dance. A heavy table and two chairs are in the way. The boys manage to lift and partly drag the table to one side of the room while the girls each lift a chair and carry it to the other side of the room. They then get into position again to practice their dance.

Once children have learned the rules of pantomime, let them pantomime the actions, movements, or moods of the characters in a story they have just heard. This kind of activity adds zest to the story and promotes closer identification with the characters.

For instance, let one child be the cook and another the scullery boy in the "Sleeping Beauty." The cook falls asleep just as he has his arm raised to cuff the ears of the scullery boy while the boy himself, in a defensive position to ward off the blow, falls asleep simultaneously.

Let the children take turns being the Emperor as he haughtily parades before his subjects, believing he is dressed in robes of lustrous magnificence.

Let the children take turns being Goldilocks as she tastes the three bowls of porridge.

Pantomime in the story hour should be used to heighten the interest in stories you tell, never to substitute for stories.

Creating a Play

If the story hour children manifest an interest in more sophisticated acting-out and if you have the time and inclination, an informal dramatization of a story can be created and performed, either as an added feature of a story hour or for a special occasion. If you want to try such a project, I recommend doing it with eight-, nine-, and ten-year-olds rather than with very small children.

First, you must search for a suitable story—one that lends itself to dramatization. The plot should contain a strong conflict, which is resolved in an interesting and satisfying way. The story line should be simple and clear-cut without complicated subplots. Description should be at a minimum, the dialogue propelling the action forward. Preferably, the setting should be in one place, but this is not mandatory. Few characters are easier to manage than many, but having few characters also means that miscellaneous jobs must be devised for all those who do not get acting parts.

The story must appeal not only to you, but also to the children. To begin with, it should be told just as any other story. Carefully note the children's reactions. Did they like the story? Did they listen with their eyes as well as their ears? Ask the children if they think it would be fun to act out the story. If their answer is "Yes," then offer to tell it again, admonishing the listeners to think about the characters in the story and to listen carefully to what each character says.

As an example of a good story to act out, let us choose "THE THREE BILLY-GOATS-GRUFF."[4]

Once upon a time there were three Billy-Goats who were to go up to the hillside to make themselves fat, and the family name of the three goats was "Gruff."

On the way up was a bridge, over a burn they had to cross; and under the bridge lived a great ugly Troll, with eyes as big as saucers and a nose as long as a poker.

First of all came the youngest Billy-Goat-Gruff to cross the bridge.

"Trip, trap; trip, trap!" went the bridge.

"WHO'S THAT tripping over my bridge?" roared the troll.

"Oh! it is only I, the tiniest Billy-Goat-Gruff; and I'm going up to the hillside to make myself fat," said the Billy-Goat, with such a small voice.

"Now, I'm coming to gobble you up," said the Troll.

"Oh, no! pray don't take me. I'm too little, that I am," said the Billy-Goat. "Wait a bit till the second Billy-Goat-Gruff comes; he's much bigger."

"Well! be off with you," said the Troll.

A little while after came the second Billy-Goat-Gruff to cross the bridge.

"Trip, Trap! Trip, Trap! Trip, Trap!" went the bridge.

"WHO'S THAT tripping over my bridge?" roared the Troll.

"Oh! it's the second Billy-Goat-Gruff, and I'm going up to the hillside to make myself fat," said the Billy-Goat, who hadn't such a small voice.

"Now, I'm coming to gobble you up," said the Troll.

"Oh, no! don't take me. Wait a little till the big Billy-Goat-Gruff comes; he's much bigger."

"Very well; be off with you," said the Troll.

But just then up came the big Billy-Goat-Gruff.

"Trip, Trap! Trip, Trap! Trip, Trap!" went the bridge, for the Billy-Goat was so heavy that the bridge creaked and groaned under him.

"WHO'S THAT tramping over my bridge?" roared the Troll.

"It's I! THE BIG BILLY-GOAT-GRUFF," said the Billy-Goat, who had a big hoarse voice of his own.

"Now, I'm coming to gobble you up," roared the Troll.

"Well, come along! I've got two spears

> And I'll poke your eyeballs out at your ears,
> I've got besides two curling-stones,
> And I'll crush you to bits, body and bones."

That was what the big Billy-Goat said; so he flew at the Troll and poked his eyes out with his horns, and crushed him to bits, body and bones, and tossed him out into the burn, and after that he went up to the hillside. There the Billy-Goats got so fat they were scarcely able to walk home again; and if the fat hasn't fallen off them, why they're still fat; and so—

> Snip, snap, snout,
> This tale's told out.

The story line is simple and clear, the characters are few and distinct, and the action occurs in one place—on and near a bridge. The dialogue is clearly spelled out, and the action is swift and dramatic.

After the second telling, invite a discussion of the story's dramatic possibilities. The discussion might go something like this:

STORYTELLER: What is the problem in this story?

A CHILD: How to get across the bridge while the Troll is underneath.

ANOTHER CHILD: Yes, the Billy-Goats want to go up to the hillside and they are afraid of the mean old ugly Troll who gobbles everybody up whenever they try to cross the bridge.

ANOTHER CHILD: They want to get rid of the Troll so they can cross the bridge any old time.

STORYTELLER: That's right. They want to feel free to go to the hillside whenever they're hungry.

A CHILD: They want to come back across the bridge too because they live on this side of the bridge.

STORYTELLER: Right! They don't want the Troll waiting for them when they return. How many characters are there?

A CHILD: Three. The three Billy-Goats-Gruff.

STORYTELLER: And?

A CHILD: Four. You didn't count the Troll.

STORYTELLER: Yes, we mustn't omit the Troll. Now how can we differentiate among the Billy-Goats?

A CHILD: They're different sizes. We could have a small boy or even a girl take the part of the littlest goat.

STORYTELLER: Yes, that's a good idea. We'll have to get three people of different sizes to play the parts of the three Gruff brother goats. And what about the Troll? Does he have to be big?

A CHILD: Not too big. He just has to be mean.

STORYTELLER: He has to *pretend* to be mean!

A CHILD: And he has to have a false face with eyes as big as saucers . . .

TWO CHILDREN: And a nose as long as a poker.

STORYTELLER: Yes, perhaps we can make masks for the Billy-Goats and the Troll. Do you think that would work?

A CHILD: Yes, but I don't see how he's going to be broken to bits?

STORYTELLER: Well, on the stage, characters are never really beaten or killed. It's all pretend. But does anyone have any idea as to how we can explain it to the audience?

A CHILD: The Billy-Goat can pretend to hit the Troll and push him off the stage.

A CHILD (to the storyteller): You could just say, "The Big Billy-Goat-Gruff broke him to bits," and then the audience would get the idea.

STORYTELLER: Yes, but perhaps as the Big Billy-Goat-Gruff struggles with the Troll, he can say, "I'll break you to bits both body and bones" and then after the Troll is supposedly tossed into the river, the Billy-Goat can say, "There, now we're rid of that horrid old Troll forever."

A CHILD: What happens to the Troll really? Does he just stay there?

STORYTELLER: Well, we'll have to work that out, won't we? The Billy-Goat-Gruff might push him off as he pretends to throw him into the river; or the Troll might roll over and curl up behind the chair—and not show his face again. But let's begin at the beginning. How can we introduce the story and let the audience know what the Billy-Goats have decided to do?

A CHILD: I know. You could have the three Billy-Goats-Gruff talking it over by themselves, saying, "Oh Gee, there isn't much good grass around here. We ought to go to the hillside on the other side of the river where there's some really good grass!"

STORYTELLER: That's a good suggestion. But before we proceed further, I suggest we read the story again and think about what needs to be said in dialogue, or conversation, that the author tells us by way of explanation.

Read the story once more while everyone concentrates on the problem. If the children are good readers, let them take turns reading the story.

STORYTELLER: Now, instead of having someone tell the audience who the characters are and where they want to go and why, can the characters do all the explaining through dialogue or conversation? That is what makes a play different from a story.

At this point, you can divide the children into small groups, each of which should try to improvise the necessary opening dialogue. You should warn the children that the Billy-Goats must not disclose to the audience how they plan to trick the Troll.

This preliminary planning and plotting out of the action need not be rushed. A pleasant experience in and of itself, it can extend to a second story hour meeting or work session. Although the dialogue need not be written out, it is permissible for each group to write out the lines that are to be spoken and to assign each speech to the appropriate actor. Even if the lines are written, I suggest you encourage naturalness and improvisation rather than strict memorization. A story hour play should remain informal and suggestive.

The end result of the children's efforts, with your help, may be something like this:

BIG BILLY-GOAT-GRUFF: Good morning, Billy-Goat brothers. I've been thinking about what we can do to get more and better food. And the only possibility I can see is for us to go up to the green hillside on the other side of the river, where we'd get lots of grass and get real fat. We must try to cross the bridge!

MIDDLE BILLY-GOAT-GRUFF: I've been thinking of that too, but I must admit I am afraid of "you know who," who lives under the bridge.

BIG BILLY-GOAT-GRUFF: Yes, I know who lives under the bridge—the ugly mean old Troll with eyes as big as saucers and a nose as long as a poker.

SMALLEST BILLY-GOAT-GRUFF: What about me? If you go across the bridge to the green hillside, I want to go too, but the Troll will surely gobble me up in one mouthful.

BIG BILLY-GOAT-GRUFF: Unless we can think of a way to get him first. We must put our heads together and make a plan.

They go into a huddle and whisper to each other.

At this point, the attention of the audience focuses on the Troll. Wearing a scary and ugly false face, he comes up from behind a rock and struts across an area of the stage indicating the length of the bridge. He says:

TROLL: Ha, ha, ha. I have scared everyone away from my bridge with my mean face and fierce voice. But I'm getting hungry. I wish some billy goats would come along. That's just what I'm ready for. Yum, yum. A billy goat would taste mighty good. Well, I'll just have to be patient and wait.

The troll goes down behind the rock.
The goats come out of their huddle.

SMALLEST BILLY-GOAT-GRUFF: Well, I'm not so sure your plan will work big brother, but I'll do as you say, if you insist.

BIG BILLY-GOAT-GRUFF: Oh, little brother, do not fear. I am sure our plan will work. And if it does, just think! We will get rid of the Troll forever, and everyone in the valley will be grateful.

SMALLEST BILLY-GOAT-GRUFF: And we'll be able to go back and forth across the bridge whenever we like?

MIDDLE BILLY-GOAT-GRUFF: Yes, we will! I have confidence in you big brother. But I won't deny I'm still scared.

SMALLEST BILLY-GOAT-GRUFF: I'm scared too. I'm the most scared because I have to go across the bridge first!

BIGGEST BILLY-GOAT-GRUFF: Don't be afraid, little brother. We will be watching you and will come to your aid if our plan doesn't work.

Presently, the Smallest Billy-Goat-Gruff approaches the bridge. His brothers stand nearby, watching him. He takes small, light steps onto the bridge saying, "Trip, trap, trip, trap, trip, trap."

The Troll peers out and says, "Who is that tripping over my bridge?"

SMALLEST BILLY-GOAT: It is I, the smallest Billy-Goat-Gruff.
TROLL: I am coming to gobble you up.
SMALL BILLY-GOAT: Oh, please don't do that. Why don't you wait for my brother? He's much bigger than I am.
TROLL: Very well, get along with you then.

And the Smallest Billy-Goat continues on and goes off the opposite side of the stage.

The middle-sized Billy-Goat now approaches and repeats the action and dialogue, following which he goes off in the same direction as the smallest Billy-Goat. Next, the Big Billy-Goat-Gruff lumbers up the bridge.

TROLL: Who is that tramping over my bridge?
BIG BILLY-GOAT-GRUFF: It is I, the Biggest Billy-Goat-Gruff.
TROLL: Well, I am coming to gobble you up!
BIG BILLY-GOAT-GRUFF: Come along then. I have two spears, and I'll poke your eyes out of your ears. I have besides two rolling stones and I'll crush you to bits both body and bones.
TROLL: Here I come!

The Troll comes out from behind the rock, and the two wrestle while the Troll cries, "Hey, not so rough! Not so fast!" And the Billy-Goat-Gruff says, "I have horns, I told you I'd crush you to bits." (They talk at the same time so that what they say isn't too important.) The Big Billy-Goat-Gruff pushes the Troll behind the rock and looks down as though he's looking into the river. "There, our plan worked and we're rid of the Troll forever and ever," and the Big Billy-Goat goes on to join his brothers.

The next scene is two days later, and the goats are going home.

BIGGEST BILLY-GOAT-GRUFF: Well, that was a good dinner!

MIDDLE BILLY-GOAT-GRUFF: And a good breakfast too!

SMALLEST BILLY-GOAT-GRUFF: And a good supper!

BIGGEST BILLY-GOAT-GRUFF: We ate all we could hold in two days, and we got pretty fat!

MIDDLE BILLY-GOAT-GRUFF: Yes, I couldn't have eaten another blade of grass. I'm so fat, I can hardly waddle!

SMALLEST BILLY-GOAT-GRUFF: I'm pretty fat too and I'm not a bit hungry.

BIG BILLY-GOAT-GRUFF: Now, the Troll is gone forever, and we won't ever be bothered with him again.

MIDDLE BILLY-GOAT-GRUFF: We can return to the green hillside whenever we get hungry.

SMALLEST BILLY-GOAT-GRUFF: We'll have to wait till this fat rolls off before we go back for more grass.

ALL THREE: Snip, snap, snout. Our play's run out.

The selection of the cast can become a creative experience for all concerned. Avoid favoritism, arbitrary judgment, or haste. Any child who wants to act should be encouraged to "try out" for a part. Even children who are timid or uncertain should be urged to participate. "Trying out" is a learning experience for all the children; they learn from each other even as they discover their own potential and limitations. You must create and maintain a friendly and warm atmosphere and look for the good points in each child.

With such a small cast in "The Three Billy-Goats-Gruff," you should try to create jobs for other eager actors so that as many children as possible can participate. One child might be the announcer who tells the audience the name of the play and the names of the characters and gives a description of the setting. Another child can be responsible for saying the rhymed lines at the end of the play,

> Snip, Snap, Snout,
> Our play's run out.

Or all the children involved in the play may say the last two lines in unison.

Another excellent way to use all available talent is to have a double cast. Each group performs on different days or on the same day if the audience is willing (and it usually is). With a double cast, if one actor fails to appear, there is a ready-made understudy, and the show can go on.

Two or more children can be assigned the task of setting the stage. Keep it simple. A chair on its side with a gray blanket thrown over it or crumpled newspapers as a cover can make an acceptable rock, just as two posts (or chairs) with a string extended between them can become a fine bridge.

You may have to take the responsibility for making the headdresses or masks, but let the children help. If this task is burdensome or if you fear the voices will be muffled behind a false face, let each child wear a sign indicating his character.

As the storyteller, you must protect the status and significance of the story hour. Acting out a story should not develop into an overwhelming project. Daily or even weekly rehearsals are unnecessary. The story is the heart of the story hour and pantomiming bits of action or acting out a scene or even the entire story are suggested means of involving the listeners and intensifying their interest in the story itself.

Puppetry in the Story Hour

Some storytellers make puppets, or help children make them, with which to act out their stories. Sometimes the dialogue is spoken by whoever manipulates the puppets; sometimes the dialogue is tape-recorded in advance and played while the show goes on. The puppets can range from simple paper-bag hand puppets, made and manipulated by children, to sophisticated papier-mâché puppets and marionettes. The time and talent of the storyteller are the big factors here. Puppets usually require a puppet theater, but can also be used by children in full view of the audience. Even though perfection of performance will probably be sacrificed, I strongly urge children's participation in any kind of dramatic activity, including puppet shows.

Other Dramatic Sources

Plays written specifically for children are also available, but I personally feel they should not be used in the story hour. That is not to imply that such plays are unworthy or inferior; they simply belong to another kind of childhood activity, which falls outside the realm of the story hour.

A play can also originate entirely among the children and need not be a dramatization of a story at all. Although I believe that children should be encouraged to create their own stories and plays, my first preference is to have them create plays from good, strong stories that have literary merit and dramatic themes. Children have much to gain from their intimate association with folk literature, fairy tales, and poetry. Playacting engenders such close association.

As we have seen, storytelling has many facets and can itself evolve into a variety of activities. It is a short step indeed from the quiet telling of "The Selfish Giant" to a rollicking drama enacted before a group of enthralled children. Storytelling can carry the storyteller and the listeners into realms of literature that spark the imagination and kindle the creative spirit. It is fun, and it is rewarding whether it remains a simple story hour or takes on aspects of creative theater.

NOTES FOR CHAPTER 5

1. Alfred, Lord Tennyson, *The Poetic and Dramatic Works of Alfred, Lord Tennyson* (Boston: Houghton Mifflin, 1898).
2. Rhoda Bacmeister, *Stories to Begin On* (New York: Dutton, 1940).
3. Harry Behn, *Windy Morning* (New York: Harcourt, 1953).
4. Peter Christen Asbjørnsen, *Popular Tales from the Norse*, translated by G. W. Dasent (New York: Putnam, 1908).

Chapter 6   PLANNING THE STORY HOUR

THE STORY HOUR is not always an hour. It may last fifteen minutes, thirty minutes, sixty minutes, or more. It is also a period of make-believe that may be remembered for days, even years. Much depends upon how you and others plan it.

Frequently, you, as a storyteller, are given a specific time and setting in which you are expected to sparkle on your own. You are asked to come to a library, a playground, a church hall, or a schoolroom, and to participate in a program that already has established characteristics. The time and the place may not entirely suit you, which makes it all the more important for you to anticipate a variety of circumstances and plan your performance accordingly.

Much depends upon the hour of the day, the age of the children, their needs, interests, tolerance, and experience in listening. Certainly, three-year-olds cannot be expected to sit quietly for a full half-hour of stories. A group of alert sixth graders, on the other hand, will easily sit through two fifteen-minute tales if the stories have action, suspense, and drama. For any group, the story hour should end before the patience of the listeners does.

Divide each story hour into segments, and let each segment provide a change of pace, a change of activity, or a change in the type of story. Sometimes you must make a quick decision to prolong or curtail the planned program. If the audience seems restive, bring the program to a speedy close even if you had planned to tell another story. When the allotted time is over, if the children insist on hearing another story, tell one more very short story or repeat a short one they had liked earlier, and then no more. It is better by far to give your audience a little less than it wants than to give too much.

The opening and closing of the story hour should have a certain amount of orderliness. It is important to begin on time and to end as close to the announced time as possible. Any adjustments during the story hour must be made by the storyteller, never by the children. You must be prepared to meet all emergencies and to adapt your program to meet the interests and experience of the children even though this might entail some last-minute changes in your plans.

As a rule, I have found the minimum time for a preschool story hour to be fifteen minutes, and a good maximum time to be thirty minutes. The minimum time for older boys and girls is still fifteen minutes but the maximum may be forty-five to sixty minutes.

How Long Should the Stories Be?

The children's interest span must be the determining factor in deciding the length of each story to be told. It is the storyteller's responsibility to recognize the group's listening tolerance and to adjust programs accordingly.

For the novice storyteller, my advice is to classify your repertoire as follows: very short stories (one to two pages), short stories (four to six pages), and fairly long stories (ten to twenty-five pages). The time required by the telling will differ from storyteller to storyteller because individual speech patterns and tempos differ. As part of your preparation, you must time your own telling of each story. Then you will be able to plan an entire program and feel secure in your timing—even with last-minute program changes.

Where Should the Story Hour Take Place?

If you could select a place for storytelling, you probably would not choose either a large school auditorium or a small hospital room. Yet you could do well in either of those places.

I have told stories to a large group of over a hundred children in an auditorium, I have told stories to a small group that sat around me (and on me) on a plot of grass in a public playground, and I have told stories to one child as we shared a comfortable rocking chair. I found happiness and satisfaction under each of those circumstances, but I believe the best situation for the *children* is a relatively small, homogeneous group, sitting quite close to the storyteller, indoors or out.

Many libraries, both school and public, have a storytelling corner or room with carpet or cushions on the floor, where children can shut out all distractions and give themselves wholly to the magic of a story. Frequently, schoolrooms have portable furniture so that chairs can be placed in a semicircle—a grouping that breaks the formality of row upon row of chairs and desks. Story time is a friendly, cozy time, and anything that the storyteller can do to promote the comfort and receptivity of the children is good. Whether you have children grouped around a campfire or sitting at desks in a classroom, you can, by your own warmth and friendliness, help create a comfortable and pleasant atmosphere.

Should Attendance Be Limited in Number, and Should Mothers Be Included?

Limiting the number of children for a story hour depends, of course, on the space available and the estimate of children who want to attend. Some librarians limit the attendance of the preschool story hour to twenty and require the children's parents to sign up in advance. Other librarians have so few children that the question of restricting attendance is nonexistent. In the first situation, the parents were excluded from the story hour; in the second, the mothers were urged to come because "they need to hear stories as much as their children do." Certainly, an audience consisting of ten children and two mothers must be handled differently from one in which there are forty children and twenty mothers. Plan, if you can, to get relatively small and homogeneous groups; but *be prepared* to take care of unusual audiences too.

Physical facilities are a paramount consideration. The need of the children to be, or not to be, near their mothers may be determined by seating arrangements or by the individual child or parent. The teacher-storyteller in a schoolroom does not have such problems. She has the same children every day, and the mothers are rarely, if ever, present. Storytellers in child-care centers and nursery schools have a fairly uniform pattern, too, even though "mother-helpers" frequently join the children and listen to the stories told.

Summer story hours in parks, recreation centers, and libraries have their own customs or regulations, and usually attendance simply cannot be limited in numbers or ages. Ten-year-olds bring their little siblings, mothers sometimes bring their neighbors' children as well as their own, and many children who just happen to be on the spot at the right moment "drop in" out of curiosity. This kind of heterogeneous group presents a real challenge to the storyteller, not only in the selection of appropriate material, but also in coping with such a large and assorted group of children. Such a situation demands stage presence; a good, strong voice; and some truly good tales. Your bag of stories will become ever richer and more adequate to the occasion as your experience grows.

Storytellers often find change frustrating, but, as a story-teller, you must *cultivate* flexibility and adaptability. You must learn to accept change as a matter of course and take it in stride. Plan your story hour as carefully as you can with the physical facilities available to you, and then try to meet all emergencies with composure.

Should the Story Hour Include "Other Attractions" Such as Music, Games, Finger Plays?

I have no single answer for the storyteller who feels the need for some assistance. Try to avoid reliance upon a crutch, but if you want to experiment with aids, do so. Just remember that you are planning a story hour and you must be the central attraction.

I have found variation among successful storytellers. One competent children's librarian plays the guitar and sings, and her paraprofessional assistant tells the stories. This librarian insists she could never hold the attention of the "big kids," ten to thirteen, in her neighborhood culture if she did not play the guitar. She also maintains that story hours are easier if there is a team of two or more. Another librarian from a different community in the same library system says she never uses music of any kind in her weekly story hour, which has an attendance of one hundred children of mixed ages.

Still another librarian who makes regular visits to nursery schools and child-care centers in a Mexican-American neighborhood takes along a Spanish-speaking translator, made available through federal funding. This librarian shows the pictures of a book to the children and tells them the story in English. The translator then takes a small group of children to a corner of the room and shows them the pictures in the same book and tells the story in Spanish. She finds she has better rapport if she "works" with four or five children at a time.

A Japanese-American storyteller working in a neighborhood in which the population is 90 percent Japanese seeks out bilingual picture-storybooks to present in her story hours. When I asked her how the non-Japanese children reacted, she laughed and said, "They like it; they're learning many Japanese words and songs."

Other storytellers show films, play records, or put on puppet shows and plays. There are strengths and weaknesses in all of these approaches. I would not categorically rule out any.

Variety in the story hour is fundamentally important. It should, however, develop out of the stories and poetry that are offered to the children. If there is music, I like it to be background for the children's activities. Better still, the children can do their own singing. If there is a puppet show, I prefer to have the children write the script, manipulate the puppets, and speak the parts. But most of all, I believe in the art of storytelling and in its intrinsic value for children. The story is the thing, and the storyteller excels when he does his thing.

There are no substitutes for stories of great and adventurous heroes, fanciful tales of fairy and elf, or the rollicking and dramatic accounts of giants, witches, and fearsome animals. Other activities—finger plays, choral speaking, acting out—are useful because they provide an opportunity for children's participation and relaxation. They afford variety in tempo and help children loosen the tensions required

103

in listening. They should be adjuncts to the storytelling program; stories must always be the heart of the story hour.

Illustrative Story Hour Plans

1. Library Story Hour for Preschoolers (ages three to four)

A library story hour for preschoolers is likely to take place in a branch of the public library. The children will come with three teachers from a child-care center two blocks from the library. There are twenty-five children. They are to come in the morning when the library is closed to the public. It is a hot summer day, but it is cool and pleasant in the library. The teachers want the children to stay in the library for thirty minutes. They will already have had juice and crackers, and when they return to the center, they will have lunch and naps. You are to have them from 10:30 until 11:00. The following program is a suggested one; infinite variations can be made.

Introduction

"Hello, children, I'm very happy that you could come to the library today. How many of you have been here before?" (Not many.) "Well, before you leave today, we'd like to take you on a little walk all around the library so that you can see all the books. Aren't these lots of books?" (Leads them into the Children's Room.) "Do you know what we call this part of the library? We call this the Children's Room because it was made just for you and other children like you. Do you see those bright cushions on the floor? Those are for you to sit on if you like. Yes, you may sit on them right now. And after a while you may each look at a picture book while you sit on your cushion.

"Does everybody have a cushion?" (Perhaps one child needs help in getting his cushion and getting seated. You or the teacher should help him.) "Now, I want to see each one of you, and I want you to be able to see me. Do you have elbow room?" (Put your hands on hips, poking out your elbows.) "And leg room?" (Let them stretch out so that they are not too close to each other and also so that each child can see you. The teachers have pinned name tags on the children for your benefit. You should try to use the child's name in addressing him.)

"I'm going to tell you a story about a little boy who wanted to plant a carrot seed." (Hold up the book so all can see it.) "You all know what carrots are, don't you? Do you like carrots? Does anybody have a garden at home?" (One child volunteers that they have a garden at school. This prompts others to comment about the garden at school.)

The Story

Tell the story of "The Carrot Seed" by Ruth Krauss, and hold the book in such a way that the children can see each picture.

"Do you have carrots growing in your garden at school?" "No," say the children. "Well," you reply, "maybe you'll be able to plant some carrot seeds one of these days." The first inclination of the novice storyteller is to ask the children if they liked the story. *Refrain* from such questions. They will answer whatever they think you want to hear. Besides, that story is over, and you should move on to the next thing that is relevant.

Finger Play

"Can you clap your hands real loud? Good! Let's play a

little clapping game. This is called, 'Follow the leader,' and you have to do just what I do and clap when I say 'clap.' O.K.? Put your hands on your head and *clap!* Put your hands on your head, on your shoulders, and *clap!* Good. Now, put your hands on your head, your shoulders, and your tummy, and *clap!* Everybody stand up" (pause while they stand). "Now, watch very closely. Put your hands on your head, your shoulders, your tummy—and your knees, and *clap!* Now—we're going to do a long one. Watch carefully. Put your hands on your head, your shoulders, your tummy, your knees—and your toes, and *clap!* Oh, that was very good. How quietly can you sit down on your cushions again?" (Whispering.)

A Poem

"A little while ago I saw a little bird fly up to the window and look inside. Did you see any birds this morning? When the days get very cold, birds look for a place to get warm. There's a poem that tells about a robin and what he does when it gets cold outside."

Speak or read "The North Wind Doth Blow."

Repeat the poem, and when the poor robin tucks his head under his wing, tell the children to put their heads under their arms. They'll all look like little robins in the snow.

A Second Story

"I'm going to show you this book about *Madeline*." Use the picture-storybook technique, and be sure to let the children look closely at the pictures. They can see the "sad" man who hurt his foot, the "winter, snow, and ice," and some will even understand about the scar on Madeline's stomach. Let them interrupt and ask questions. When all the questions are answered and they've had a good chance to see the pictures, ask them if they want to hear it again. This time do it more quickly, stressing the rhyme and hastening the tempo.

Time-out Stretch

"Let's walk all around the library and see all the books. Perhaps we can listen to music while we go for our walk. Shall we walk in two's the way you did when you came to the library? Good!" They all stand up. You play a marching record with a good beat, and you lead them around while their teachers follow along behind.

Conclusion

"Let's each one sit down on a bright cushion. I want you to have a few minutes to look at some very special books. They have many pictures, and you can hold the books and look at the pictures. You sit on your cushion, and your teachers and I will give you each a book to look at. And while you're looking, I'll put another record on the record player, and you can listen to the music with your ears while your eyes are busy looking at the pictures." Give them the books that have already been set aside.

"Some day, maybe your Mommy will bring you to the library, and she may borrow some books for you to take home for a while and then bring back another day." (After three to five minutes of browsing they are ready to leave.)

"Children, you've made me very happy by coming to visit me in the library. I hope you'll come again, and we'll have more stories and games. Goodbye!" They leave their books on the table as they pass it.

2. A Girl Scout Troop Story Hour

There are fifteen girls, ten to twelve years old, who are attending a cookout picnic in a park. Before the cookout, they played baseball for a half hour and then participated fully in the preparation of the food, setting the table, and so on. They have now finished their supper and "tidying up" and are ready for a quiet time, a song or two, and their customary friendship ritual.

There are four adults: the troop leader, two "extra" mothers, and you, the co-leader. The troop leader likes to lead the games and songs, the extra mothers have supervised the preparation of the food, and your responsibility is to tell a story.

Introduction

"Girls, being out here in this beautiful park and having eaten such a wonderful dinner makes me think of a story that is just the opposite of all this. Instead of bright sunshine and green grass and trees, this story is about a cold snowy day—a blizzard, in fact; and instead of a happy bunch of girls, it's about a lonely and scared boy—but it isn't really sad—it's just different."

The First Story

Tell the story of "Zlateh the Goat" by Isaac Bashevis Singer. Pause for a moment or two at the end of the story, and then laughingly say:

Second Story

"Oh, I know a short, short, very silly story. Do you know what a "noodlehead" is? Well, simpletons and fools are noodleheads and you never know when or where you will find one. I found a whole book of noodlehead stories, and they're quite funny. They were collected from all over the world! Every country has its share of noodlehead stories. This one is called, 'A New Way to Boil Eggs' by Jagendorf, and it's about a couple of noodleheads in Ireland."

Conclusion

After the story, the girls sing one or two of their usual songs; then they form a circle and have their brief, quiet ritual ceremony of friendship, and the outing is over.

3. A Summer Story Hour in the Public Library

The story hour is a regular weekly event in a suburban branch library. There is an average attendance of fifty to seventy-five children, covering a wide age range.

Tables are pushed to one side of the children's room, and small chairs are used around the periphery of the area for those who want them, but most of the children prefer to sit on the floor.

The biggest problem in this situation is to find stories of universal appeal in order to hold the attention of all the children.

Just before story time, your assistant puts a record on to provide background music, which hopefully will have a calming effect on the children. Try to get them seated and settled as quickly as you can without looking or sounding "pushed." Keep your "cool." Try to have the smallest children sit right in front, as close to you as feasible. Begin the minute the children are seated even though a few latecomers may still straggle in. The music can be turned off as soon as you begin to speak.

Introduction

"Hello boys and girls. Welcome to our summer story hour. I'm glad you could come today, and I hope that after the program you'll find some good books to take home. We have put some books on this table that might interest many of you." (Indicate a display of bright-jacketed books.) "Some are brand new books, and some are old favorites that many boys and girls have liked. And we've also included some attractive picture-storybooks for the very little people." (Hold up one or two.)

"I see that many of you have brought your little sisters and brothers."

The First Story

"My first story is for them, but they won't mind if you listen."

Tell "The Old Woman and the Pig."

The Second Story

"I am sure that some of you have heard or read the story of Puss in Boots." (Hold up a copy of Marcia Brown's *Puss in Boots.*) "Well, I'm going to tell you a story that is very much like *Puss in Boots,* but instead of a cat, it is about a very sly and clever fox. It's called 'The Miller King,' and it's from this book of Armenian folktales called *Once There Was and Was Not* by Virginia Tashjian." (Hold up the book so all can see it. After the story, place it on the display table with the other books that children may borrow.)

Pantomime

"Now, I want you to watch me very carefully and see if you can guess what I am doing." (Introduce pantomime by acting out drinking a cup of coffee.) "Can you tell me what I was doing? Drinking something, yes! Now tell me what you think I'm drinking and if it's hot or cold, and if it tastes good or bad." (This time your pantomime must indicate that your coffee is not only *very hot,* but it is also too strong and bitter. After the first taste, add cream and sugar, and indicate by your facial expression that the coffee is now palatable. The children guess successfully what you have done.)

"This kind of pretending is called pantomime. It's fun to try to make people recognize what you're doing or thinking. There are two rules for this game. One is that you yourself must know exactly what you're pretending to do, and the other rule is that you must not talk. Would you like to try doing some pantomime? All right. Can you pretend you're sewing? Don't prick your finger with the needle! Good! Pretend you're very sleepy, but you're trying to stay awake. Now, one more. Pretend a bee is hovering around you and you're afraid it will sting you. You can't get up and run. You must stay right where you are. Very, very good! I noticed a few of you are such good pantomimists I'm going to ask you to come up here in front and do your pantomime again so everyone can see you." (Select three of the best performers and have them take turns. Each child repeats one of the three exercises. While they return to their places, you pick up a copy of A. A. Milne's *When We Were Very Young* from the display table.)

"Pantomime is fun, isn't it. Maybe you can try one with your family at home tonight. Make them guess what you're pretending to do."

Poetry Reading

"This little book has some wonderful story poems in it. Many of them are about a little boy named Christopher

Robin, but some are about other people too." (Read "Half-way Down," and "The King's Breakfast.")

(Time is running on, and you must make a decision as to whether to tell two more short stories, one story, or no more at all. If only one, tell "Mollie Whuppie"; if two, add "Nail Soup."

Conclusion

"Our story hour for today is over, but you may stay as long as you like. You may want to look at books, to read, or check out a couple of books to take home. Thank you for coming, and come again next Thursday afternoon."

A carefully planned story hour program implies appropriate selection of stories and other materials; adequate preparation and timing of each selection to be used, as well as one or two extra items to hold in reserve; and ample physical facilities to assure the comfort and interest of each child in attendance. Leave nothing to chance. Even if the unexpected occurs and an interruption is unavoidable, try to rise above it and follow your plan, or change it as smoothly as possible. If your plan is well made, if you are well prepared, and if you enjoy children, any untimely event will be surmounted, and you will be able to maintain your dignity and charm. Good telling!

Chapter 7 BIBLIOGRAPHIES

A GOOD storyteller never stops searching for good stories. You learn your way around, and just when you believe you have seen all the best books, you are surprised to find a story that is different, that is freshly illustrated, that captivates your attention. It's a never-ending delight.

If I were to attempt a detailed bibliography for storytellers, it would make a very long book. Instead, I want to present a few lists that will reveal some of the choices.

The lists I offer you in this chapter are highly selective. I have personally chosen each book.

Every storyteller needs background learning the better to appreciate the stories one encounters. There are books that tell about children and their literature, as well as books of poetry, essays, criticism, and folklore, that contribute to a storyteller's grasp and appreciation of this entire subject. There are periodicals that deal with children and their educational and emotional needs and some that focus on children's literature in particular. There are published bibliographies and indexes of stories and poems that are ready reference guides. There are commentaries by anthologists to assist the storyteller in understanding and following the whole sweep of children's literature.

Children's literature is not to be separated from the broad, generic term *literature,* for its standards of quality, creativity, and universality are the same as for any body of literature. Still, it has a special history and development with which the storyteller should be familiar. The books in this section will enrich your background, and the periodicals will keep you abreast of new trends and new books in the field of children's literature.

BACKGROUND BOOKS

Although some of the collections of stories in the section on background books contain tales that might be used with children, most would need to be retold in simpler language and/or modified to meet children's comprehension. For example, the Perrault stories listed further on, which are well-known fairy stories, were originally told to adults and contain more sophisticated, adult overtones than children need. The Zeitlin tales are marvelous in their detail, but they are far too lengthy for story hour requirements.

Aesop. *Aesop: Five Centuries of Illustrated Fables.* Selected by John J. McKendrey. New York: The Metropolitan Museum of Art, 1964. Distributed by New York Graphic Society, Greenwich, Conn.

Anderson, William Davis. *A New Look at Children's Literature* (by) William D. Anderson (and) Patrick Groff. Bibliography by Ruth Robinson. Belmont, Calif.: Wadsworth, 1972.

Arbuthnot, May Hill. *Children and Books.* 4th edition. Chicago: Scott, Foresman, 1972.

Asbjørnsen, Peter Christen, and Moe, Jørgen. *Norwegian Folk Tales.* From the Collection of Asbjørnsen and Moe. Illustrated by Eric Werenskiold and Theodore Kittlesen. Translated by Pat Shaw Iversen and Carl Norman. Oslo: Dreyers Forlag. n.d. [1960]

Behn, Harry. *Chrysalis; Concerning Children and Poetry.* New York: Harcourt, Brace and World, 1968.

Botkin, Benjamin A., ed. *A Treasury of American Folklore; Stories, Ballads, and Traditions of the People* . . . New York: Crown, 1944.

Broderick, Dorothy M. *Image of the Black in Children's Fiction.* New York: Bowker, 1973.

Bulfinch, Thomas. *Bulfinch's Mythology; The Age of Fable; The Age of Chivalry; Legends of Charlemagne.* 1 vol. New York: The Modern Library, n.d.

Children's Book Council, New York. *Children's Books; Awards and Prizes.* Compiled and edited by Christine Stawicki. 1973 ed. New York: Children's Book Council, 1973.

Chukovsky, Kornei. *From Two to Five.* Translated and edited by Miriam Morton . . . Berkeley: University of California Press, 1968.

Cianciolo, Patricia Jean. *Picture Books for Children.* Patricia Jean Cianciolo, Editor, and the Picture Book Committee, Subcommittee of the National Council of Teachers of English, Elementary Booklist Committee. Chicago: American Library Association, 1973.

Cook, Elizabeth. *The Ordinary and the Fabulous; an Introduction to Myths, Legends and Fairy Tales for Teachers and Storytellers.* London: Cambridge University Press, 1969.

Delarue, Paul, ed. *The Borzoi Book of French Folk Tales.* Selected and edited by Paul Delarue. Translated by Austin E. Fife. Illustrated by Warren Chappell. New York: Alfred A. Knopf, 1956.

Dickinson, Emily. *Poems.* First and Second Series edited by Mabel Loomis Todd and T. W. Higginson. Illustrated by Leon Jacobson. Introduction by Carl Van Doren. Cleveland: World Publishing Co., 1948.

Duff, Annis. *Bequest of Wings; a Family's Pleasure with Books.* New York: Viking Press, 1944.

———— *Longer Flight.* New York: Viking Press, 1955.

Eberhard, Wolfram, ed. and tr. *Folktales of China.* Revised edition. Chicago: University of Chicago Press, 1965. (First published in 1937 under the title *Chinese Fairy and Folk Tales.*)

Eckenstein, Lina. *Comparative Studies in Nursery Rhymes* . . . London: Duckworth, 1906. Reissued by Singing Tree Press (Detroit), 1968.

Ellis, Alec. *How to Find Out About Children's Literature.* 3rd edition. Oxford, Eng.; Elmsford, N.Y.: Pergamon Press, 1973.

Frost, Robert. *Complete Poems of Robert Frost.* New York: Holt, Rinehart and Winston, 1964.

Funk and Wagnalls. *Standard Dictionary of Folklore, Mythology and Legend.* Edited by Maria Leach. 2 vols. New York: Funk & Wagnalls, 1949–1950.

Gaer, Joseph. *Holidays Around the World.* Illustrated by Anne Marie Jauss. Boston: Little, Brown and Co., 1953.

Hamilton, Edith. *Mythology.* Illustrated by Steele Savage. Boston: Little, Brown and Co., 1942.

Haviland, Virginia. *Children and Literature; Views and Reviews.* Glenview, Ill.: Scott, Foresman, 1973.

Hazard, Paul. *Books, Children, and Men* . . . Translated by Marguerite Mitchell. 4th edition. Boston: The Horn Book, Inc., 1960.

Hoffman, Miriam, comp. *Authors and Illustrators of Children's Books; Writings on Their Lives and Works* by Miriam Hoffman and Eva Samuels. New York: Bowker, 1972.

Hurlimann, Bettina. *Picture-Book World.* Modern Picture-books for Children from Twenty-four Countries with a

Bio-bibliographical Supplement by Elizabeth Waldman. Translated and edited by Brian W. Alderson. Cleveland: World Publishing Co., 1969.

Jan, Isabelle. *On Children's Literature*. Edited by Catherine Storr. With a Preface by Anne Pellowski. New York: Schocken Books, 1974.

Joseph, Stephen M., ed. *The Me Nobody Knows; Children's Voices from the Ghetto*. New York: World Publishing Co., 1969.

Kingman, Lee, and others, comps. *Illustrators of Children's Books 1957–1966*. Boston: The Horn Book, Inc., 1968.

Lanes, Selma G. *Down the Rabbit Hole; Adventures and Misadventures in the Realm of Children's Literature*. New York: Atheneum, 1971.

Lanier, Sidney, ed. *The Boy's King Arthur; Sir Thomas Malory's History of King Arthur and His Knights of the Round Table* . . . Illustrated by N. C. Wyeth. New York: Charles Scribner's Sons, 1924; 1952.

Lonsdale, Bernard J., and MacKintosh, Helen K. *Children Experience Literature*. New York: Random House, 1973.

Mahoney, Bertha E., and others, comps. *Illustrators of Children's Books, 1744–1945*. Boston: The Horn Book Inc., 1947.

Marshak, Samuel. *At Life's Beginning; Some Pages of Reminiscence*. Translated (from the Russian) by Katherine Hunter Blair . . . Illustrated by G. Philippovsky. New York: E. P. Dutton, 1964.

Meigs, Cornelia Lynde, and others. *A Critical History of Children's Literature*. New York: Macmillan, 1953.

Mother Goose. *The Annotated Mother Goose; Nursery Rhymes Old and New*. Arranged and explained by William S. Baring-Gould and Ceil Baring-Gould. Illustrated by Walter Crane, Randolph Caldecott, Kate Greenaway, Arthur Rackham, Maxfield Parrish, and early historical woodcuts. New York: Bramhall House, 1962.

O'Faolain, Eileen. *Irish Sagas and Folk-Tales*. Retold by Eileen O'Faolain. Illustrated by Joan Kiddell-Monroe. New York: Oxford University Press, 1954.

Opie, Iona and Peter, eds. *The Oxford Dictionary of Nursery Rhymes*. Oxford: Oxford University Press, 1951.

Painter, Helen W., ed. *Reaching Children and Young People Through Literature*. Newark, Delaware: International Reading Association, 1971.

Perrault, Charles. *Perrault's Complete Fairy Tales*. Translated from the French by A. E. Johnson and others. Illustrated by W. Heath Robinson. London: Constable & Co., Ltd.; New York: Dodd, Mead, 1961.

Quayle, Eric. *The Collector's Book of Children's Books*. Photographs by Gabriel Monro. New York: Clarkson N. Potter, Inc., 1971. Distributed by Crown Publishers.

Robinson, Evelyn Rose, ed. *Readings About Children's Literature* . . . New York: David McKay, 1966.

Roethke, Theodore. *The Collected Poems of Theodore Roethke*. Garden City, N.Y.: Doubleday, 1966.

Ross, Eulalie Steinmetz. *The Spirited Life; Bertha Mahony Miller and Children's Books*. Selected Bibliography compiled by Virginia Haviland. Boston: The Horn Book, Inc., 1973.

Russ, Lavinia. *The Girl on the Floor Will Help You*. Illustrated by Mircea Vasiliu. New York: Doubleday, 1969.

Sayers, Frances Clarke. *Summoned by Books: Essays and Speeches*. Compiled by Marjeanne Jensen Blinn. New York: Viking Press, 1965.

Smith, Lillian H. *The Unreluctant Years; a Critical Approach to Children's Literature*. Chicago: American Library Association, 1953.

Thompson, Stith. *The Folktale*. New York: The Dryden Press, 1946.

Townsend, John R. *A Sense of Story; Essays on Contemporary Writers for Children*. Philadelphia: Lippincott, 1971.

Viguers, Ruth Hill, and others, comps. *Illustrators of Children's Books 1945–1956*. A Supplement to *Illustrators of Children's Books 1744–1945*. Boston: The Horn Book, Inc., 1958.

———— *Margin for Surprise*. Boston: Little, Brown, 1964.

Wilson, Barbara Ker. *Scottish Folk-Tales and Legends*. Retold by Barbara Ker Wilson. Illustrated by Joan Kiddell-Monroe. New York: Oxford University Press, 1960.

Zeitlin, Ida. *Skazki: Tales and Legends of Old Russia*. Illustrated by Theodore Nadejen. New York: Farrar & Rinehart, 1936.

PERIODICALS

American Education. Published ten times a year including January-February and August-September issues. United States Department of Health, Education, and Welfare/ Office of Education, Washington, D.C.

Bulletin of the Center for Children's Books. Published monthly by the University of Chicago Press, 5801 Ellis Ave., Chicago, Ill. 60637.

Childhood Education. Journal of the Association for Childhood Education International. Published monthly October through May. 3615 Wisconsin Ave., N.W., Washington, D.C. 20016.

Elementary English. The official journal of the Elementary Section of the National Council of Teachers of English. Published monthly October through May. National Council of Teachers of English, 1111 Kenyon Rd. Urbana, Ill. 61801.

The Hornbook Magazine. Published six times a year in February, April, June, August, October, and December by the Horn Book, Inc., 585 Boylston St., Boston, Mass. 02116.
Top of the News. Published November, January, April, and June by the Children's Services Division and the Young Adult Services Division of the American Library Association, 50 E. Huron St., Chicago, Ill. 60611.

BOOK LISTS AND INDEXES

The following bibliographies and indexes will be found in most public, college, and school libraries. You may wish to purchase one or more of the bibliographies for your own use as you begin to build your repertoire. Even though you must do your own searching for stories to tell, you will find the bibliographies issued by public libraries such as the New York, Baltimore, and Westchester libraries extremely helpful. The bibliographies published by the Library of Congress are especially well annotated and beautifully illustrated.

American Library Association. *Let's Read Together: Books for Family Enjoyment.* 3rd edition. Selected and annotated by a special committee of the National Congress of Parents and Teachers and the Children's Services Division of the American Library Association. Chicago, 1969.

——— *Subject and Title Index to Short Stories for Children.* Compiled by a subcommittee of ALA Editorial Committee . . . Chicago: American Library Association, 1955.

——— *Subject Index to Poetry for Children and Young People.* Compiled by Violet Sell and others. Chicago: American Library Association, 1957.

Association of Librarians of Northern California: San Francisco Public Library . . . *Pre-School Story Time for Chil-*

dren, *Ages 3–5*. Order from Cynthia King, 2420 Mariposa St., Fresno, Calif. 93721.

Brewton, John E., and Sara W., comps. *Index to Children's Poetry; a Title, Subject, Author, and First Line Index to Poetry in Collections for Children and Youth*. New York: H. W. Wilson Co., 1942.

———— *Index to Children's Poetry* . . . First Supplement . . . New York: H. W. Wilson Co., 1954.

———— and Blackburn, G. Meredith III, comps. *Index to Poetry for Children and Young People, 1964–1969* . . . New York: H. W. Wilson Co., 1972.

Cathon, Laura E., and others, eds. *Stories to Tell to Children*. 8th edition . . . Pittsburgh: University of Pittsburgh Press, 1974.

Eastman, Mary Huse. *Index to Fairy Tales, Myths and Legends*. 2nd edition. Boston: F. W. Faxon Co., 1926.

———— *Index to Fairy Tales, Myths and Legends; Supplement*. Boston: F. W. Faxon Co., 1937.

———— *Index to Fairy Tales, Myths and Legends; Second Supplement*. Boston: F. W. Faxon Co., 1952.

Foster, Joanna, comp. *How to Conduct Effective Picture Book Programs; a Handbook* . . . New York State: Westchester Library System. Distributed by The Children's Book Council, New York.

Greene, Ellin, comp. *Stories: A List of Stories to Tell and to Read Aloud*. New York: The New York Public Library, 1965.

Hardendorff, Jeanne B., ed. *Stories to Tell; a List of Stories with Annotations*. Baltimore: Enoch Pratt Free Library, 1965.

Haviland, Virginia, comp. . . . *Children and Poetry; a Selective, Annotated Bibliography* . . . Washington, D.C.: The Library of Congress, 1969.

———— *Children's Books of International Interest; a Selection from Four Decades of American Publishing.* Chicago: American Library Association, 1972.

Ireland, Norma Olin. *Index to Fairy Tales, 1949–1972; Including Folklore, Legends, & Myths in Collections* . . . Westwood, Mass.: F. W. Faxon Co., Inc., 1973.

Kujoth, Jean Spealman. *Best-Selling Children's Books.* Metuchen, N.J.: Scarecrow Press, 1973.

Pellowski, Anne. *The World of Children's Literature.* New York: R. R. Bowker Co., 1968.

Quinnam, Barbara, comp. *Fables from Incunabula to Modern Picture Books: A Selective Bibliography* . . . Washington, D.C.: The Library of Congress, 1966.

Ullom, Judith C., comp. *Folklore of the North American Indians; an Annotated Bibliography* . . . Washington, D.C.: The Library of Congress, 1969.

COMMENTARIES by ANTHOLOGISTS
AND
THEIR ANTHOLOGIES

For the storyteller who has not had a formal course in children's literature, any one of the anthologies included here will be helpful. The compilers have prefaced the various sections of their anthologies with an explanatory summary of the history and development of each particular type of literature, for example, Mother Goose, Folk Tales, Poetry, and so on. The explanatory discussion in the Johnson, Sickels, and Sayers anthology is particularly recommended. The Nelson volume is unique in that the compiler has deliberately made a comparison between the good and the bad in children's literature—with examples of each juxtaposed. All these works contain a wide assortment of children's literature—old and new—and the arrangement indicates the relationship of each genre to the whole spectrum of children's literature.

Arbuthnot, May Hill. *The Arbuthnot Anthology of Children's Literature*. A single volume edition of *Time for Poetry*; *Time for Fairy Tales (Old and New)*; *and Time for True Tales (and Almost True)*. Chicago: Scott, Foresman, 1961.

Huber, Miriam Blanton. *Stories and Verse for Children*. 3rd edition. New York: Macmillan, 1965.

Johnson, Edna; Sickels, Evelyn R.; and Sayers, Frances Clarke. *Anthology of Children's Literature*. 4th edition. . . . Boston: Houghton Mifflin, 1970.

Nelson, Mary Ann. *A Comparative Anthology of Children's Literature*. New York: Holt, Rinehart and Winston, 1972.

WHERE TO LOOK FOR STORIES TO TELL

Collections

Aesop. *The Fables of Aesop*. Edited by Joseph Jacobs. New York: Macmillan, 1962.

Ainsworth, Ruth. *The Phantom Cyclist and Other Ghost Stories*. Illustrated by Antony Maitland. Chicago: Follett, 1974.

Andersen, Hans Christian. *The Complete Fairy Tales and Stories*. Translated by Eric Haugaard. Garden City, N.Y.: Doubleday, 1974.

Arbuthnot, May Hill. *Time for Fairy Tales Old and New*. Illustrated by John Averill and others. Revised edition. Chicago: Scott, Foresman, 1961.

―――― and Taylor, Mark, comps. *Time for Old Magic*. Illustrated by John Averill and others. Glenview, Ill.: Scott, Foresman, 1970.

Asbjørnsen, P. C. and Moe, Jørgen E. *East of the Sun and West of the Moon, and Other Tales*. Collected by Asbjørnsen and Moe. Illustrated by Tom Vroman . . . New York: Macmillan, 1963.

Authors' Choice 2. Stories. An Anthology of Stories Chosen by Eighteen Distinguished Writers . . . New York: Thomas Y. Crowell, 1974.

Babbitt, Ellen C. *Jataka Tales; Animal Stories*. Retold by Ellen C. Babbitt. Illustrated by Ellsworth Young. New York: Appleton-Century-Crofts, 1912, 1940.

Birch, Cyril. *Chinese Myths and Fantasies*. Retold by Cyril Birch. Illustrated by Joan Kiddell-Monroe. New York: Henry Z. Walck, 1961.

Bonnet, Leslie. *Chinese Folk and Fairy Tales*. Illustrated by Maurice Brevannes. (Series: Folk and Fairy Tales from Many Lands) New York: G. P. Putnam's Sons, 1958.

Bowman, James C. *Pecos Bill; the Greatest Cowboy of All Time*. Boston: Houghton Mifflin, 1937.

Brown, Michael, ed. *A Cavalcade of Sea Legends*. Illustrated by Krystyna Turska. New York: Henry Z. Walck, 1971.

Chase, Richard, ed. *Grandfather Tales; American-English Folk Tales*. Selected and edited by Richard Chase. Illustrated by Berkeley Williams, Jr. Boston: Houghton Mifflin, 1948.

——— *The Jack Tales*. Told by R. M. Ward and his kindred in the Beech Mountain section of Western North Carolina . . . Illustrated by Berkeley Williams, Jr. Boston: Houghton Mifflin, 1943.

Chaucer, Geoffrey. *Tales from Chaucer*. Retold by Eleanor Farjeon. Illustrated by Marjorie Walters. New York: Oxford University Press, 1959.

Colum, Padraic. *Legends of Hawaii*. Illustrated by Don Forrer. New Haven: Yale University Press, 1937.

Darrell, Margery, ed. *Once Upon a Time; the Fairy Tale World of Arthur Rackham*. New York: Viking Press, 1972.

De la Mare, Walter, *Collected Stories for Children*. Illustrated by Robin Jacques. London: Faber & Faber, n.d.

Evans, Pauline Rush, ed. *Best Book of Fun and Nonsense*. Illustrated by Charles McCurry and George Wilde. Garden City, N.Y.: Doubleday, 1964.

Fenner, Phyllis R., comp. *Time to Laugh: Funny Tales from Here and There*. Illustrated by Henry C. Pitz. New York: Alfred A. Knopf, 1942.

Field, Edward. *Eskimo Songs and Stories*. Collected by Knud Rasmussen on the Fifth Thule Expedition. Selected and translated by Edward Field. Illustrated by Kiakshuk and Pudlo. New York: Dell, 1973.

Gaer, Joseph. *The Fables of India*. Illustrated by Randy Monk. Boston: Little, Brown, 1955.

Gág, Wanda. *More Tales from Grimm*. Freely translated and illustrated by Wanda Gág. London: Faber & Faber, 1962.

—— *Tales from Grimm*. Freely translated and illustrated by Wanda Gág. New York: Coward-McCann, 1936.

Gates, Doris. *Two Queens of Heaven: Aphrodite and Demeter*. Illustrated by Trina Schart Hyman. New York: Viking Press, 1974.

—— *The Warrior Goddess Athena*. Illustrated by Don Bolognese. New York: Viking Press, 1972.

Ginsburg, Mirra. *The Lazies; Tales of the Peoples of Russia*. Translated and edited by Mirra Ginsburg. Illustrated by Marian Parry. New York: Macmillan, 1973.

—— *One Trick Too Many; Fox Stories from Russia*. Translated by Mirra Ginsburg. Illustrated by Helen Siegl. New York: Dial Press, 1973.

Green, Roger Lancelyn, ed. *A Cavalcade of Magicians*. Illustrated by Victor Ambrus. New York: Henry Z. Walck, 1973.

Grimm, Jakob Ludwig and Wilhelm Karl. *Grimm's Fairy Tales*. Illustrated by Arthur Rackham. New York: Viking Press, 1973.

Guirma, Frederic. *Tales of Mogho; African Stories from Upper Volta*. New York: Macmillan, 1971.

Harper, Wilhelmina. *The Gunniwolf and Other Merry Tales*. Selected by Wilhelmina Harper. Illustrated by Kate Seredy. Philadelphia: David McKay, 1936.

Haskett, Edythe Rance, comp. *Some Gold, a Little Ivory; Country Tales from Ghana and the Ivory Coast*. Collected, edited, and illustrated by Edythe Rance Haskett. New York: John Day, 1971.

Haviland, Virginia, comp. *The Fairy Tale Treasury*. Illustrated by Raymond Briggs. New York: Coward, McCann & Geoghegan, 1972.

Hodges, Margaret, ed. *Tell It Again; Great Tales from Around the World*. Illustrated by Joan Berg. New York: Dial Press, 1963.

Hosford, Dorothy. *Thunder of the Gods*. Illustrated by Claire and George Louden. New York: Holt, Rinehart and Winston, 1952.

Hutchinson, Veronica S., comp. *Chimney Corner Stories; Tales for Little Children*. Collected and retold by Veronica Hutchinson. Illustrated by Lois Lenski. New York: Minton, Balch, 1925.

Jacobs, Joseph, ed. *Celtic Folk and Fairy Tales*. Selected and edited by Joseph Jacobs. Illustrated by John D. Batten. New York: G. P. Putnam's Sons, n.d.

———— *English Fairy Tales*. Collected by Joseph Jacobs. Illustrated by John D. Batten. 3rd edition revised. New York: G. P. Putnam's Sons, n.d.

Jagendorf, Moritz A. *King of the Mountains; a Treasury of Latin American Folk Stories*. New York: Vanguard Press, 1960.

———— *New England Bean-Pot; American Folk Stories to Read and to Tell*. Illustrated by Donald McKay. New York: Vanguard Press, 1948.

———— *Noodlehead Stories Around the World*. New York: Vanguard Press, 1957.

———— *The Priceless Cats, and Other Italian Folk Stories*. New York: Vanguard Press, 1956.

———— *Tyll Ulenspiegel's Merry Pranks*. Illustrated by Fritz Eichenberg. New York: Vanguard Press, 1938.

Jiménez, Juan Ramón. *Platero and I*. Translated by Eloise Roach. Illustrated by Jo Alys Downs. Austin: University of Texas Press, 1957.

Kipling, Rudyard. *Just So Stories*. Illustrated by the author. Garden City, N.Y.: Doubleday, 1907.

Lang, Andrew. *Tales of Troy and Greece*. Illustrated by Edward Bawden. London: Faber & Faber, n.d.

Leach, Maria. *Noodles, Nitwits, and Numskulls*. Illustrated by Kurt Werth. New York: World, 1961.

—— *The Rainbow Book of American Folk Tales and Legends*. Cleveland: World, 1958.

Leodhas, Sorche Nic. *Thistle and Thyme; Tales and Legends from Scotland*. Illustrated by Evaline Ness. New York: Holt, Rinehart and Winston, 1962.

Luckhardt, Mildred Corell, comp. *Spooky Tales About Witches, Ghosts, Goblins, Demons, and Such*. Illustrated by Ralph McDonald. New York: Abingdon Press, 1972.

Lyons, Grant. *Tales the People Tell in Mexico*. Illustrated by Andrew Antal . . . New York: Messner, 1972.

McDowell, Robert Eugene, comp. *Third World Voices for Children*. Edited by Robert E. McDowell and Edward Lavitt. Illustrated by Barbara Kohn Isaac. New York: Odakai Books, 1971.

MacManus, Seumas. *In Chimney Corners; Merry Tales of Irish Folklore* . . . Garden City, N.Y.: Doubleday, 1919. o.p.

Njururi, Ngumbu. *Agikuyu Folk Tales*. London: Oxford University Press, 1966.

Perrault, Charles. *Perrault's Fairy Tales*. Translated from the French by Sasha Moorsom. Illustrated by Landa Crommelynck. Garden City, N.Y.: Doubleday, 1972.

Sandburg, Carl. *Rootabaga Stories*. Illustrated by Maud and Miska Petersham. New York: Harcourt, Brace, 1923.

Scofield, Elizabeth. *Hold Tight, Stick Tight; a Collection of Japanese Folk Tales*. Illustrated by K. Wakana. Palo Alto, Calif.: Kodansha International, 1966.

Serwadda, W. Moses. *Songs and Stories from Uganda*. Illustrated by Leo and Diane Dillon. Translated and edited by Hewitt Pantaleoni. New York: Thomas Y. Crowell, 1974.

Sherlock, Philip M. *Anansi, the Spider Man; Jamaican Folk Tales*. Told by Philip M. Sherlock. Illustrated by Marcia Brown. New York: Thomas Y. Crowell, 1954.

Singer, Isaac Bashevis. *The Fools of Chelm and Their History*. Illustrated by Uri Shulevitz. Translated by the author and Elizabeth Shub. New York: Farrar, Straus & Giroux, 1973.

———— *Zlateh the Goat, and Other Stories*. Illustrated by Maurice Sendak. Translated from the Yiddish by the author and Elizabeth Shub. New York: Harper & Row, 1966.

Spicer, Dorothy Gladys. *The Kneeling Tree, and Other Folk Tales from the Middle East*. New York: Coward-McCann, 1971.

Stanovsky, Vladislav. *The Fairy Tale Tree; Stories from All Over the World*. Retold by Vladislav Stanovsky. Illustrated by Stanislav Kolibal. Translated by Jean Layton. New York: G. P. Putnam's Sons, 1961.

Tashjian, Virginia A. *Once There Was and Was Not: Armenian Tales*. Retold by Virginia Tashjian. Illustrated by Nonny Hogrogian. Boston: Little, Brown, 1966.

Tolstoy, Leo. *Twenty-two Russian Tales for Young Children, by Leo Tolstoy*. Selected, translated, and with an afterword by Miriam Morton. Illustrated by Eros Keith. New York: Simon & Schuster, 1969.

Toth, Marian Davies. *Tales from Thailand*. Illustrated by Supee Pasutanavin. Rutland, Vt.: Charles E. Tuttle, 1971.

Vinci, Leonardo da. *Fables of Leonardo da Vinci*. Interpreted and translated by Bruno Nardini. Introduction by Margaret Meek. Illustrated by Adriana Saviozzi Mazza. Northbrook, Ill.: Hubbard Press, 1972.

Uchida, Yoshiko. *The Dancing Kettle and Other Japanese Folk Tales*. Retold by Yoshiko Uchida. New York: Harcourt, Brace & World, 1949.

Wiggin, Kate Douglas, and Smith, Nora A. *Tales of Laughter*. Garden City, N.Y.: Doubleday, 1926.

Wilde, Oscar. *The Happy Prince and Other Stories*. Illustrated by Peggy Fortnum. New York: Franklin Watts, 1968.

Wilson, Barbara Ker. *Fairy Tales of Mexico* . . . Retold by Barbara Ker Wilson. Illustrated by G. W. Miller. London: Cassell, 1960.

Special Stories

Every story in the following list is a story that I personally like well enough to tell. As I indicated in the first chapter, the story you select must be one that appeals to you in a very special way. You must feel a kinship to it and a genuine desire to spend the time necessary to learn it. I cannot choose stories for anyone but myself and the audiences I hope to reach. And you must choose the same way.

These books are distinguished by their artistry in illustration. A few are picture books without much text or plot; but most can be told as picture-storybooks.

Alden, Raymond MacDonald. *Why the Chimes Rang*. Illustrated by Rafaello Busoni. New York: Bobbs-Merrill, 1954.

Alexander, Lloyd. *The Four Donkeys*. Illustrated by Lester Abrams. New York: Holt, Rinehart and Winston, 1972.

Andersen, Hans Christian. *The Nightingale*. Translated by Eva Le Gallienne. Illustrated by Nancy Ekholm Burkert. New York: Harper & Row, 1965.

Aruego, José and Ariane. *A Crocodile's Tale; a Philippine Folk Story*. New York: Charles Scribner's Sons, 1972.

Barth, Edna. *Jack O'Lantern*. Illustrated by Paul Galdone. New York: Seabury Press, 1974.

Bemelmans, Ludwig. *Madeline*. Illustrated by the author. New York: Simon & Schuster, 1954.

Berson, Harold. *The Boy, the Baker, the Miller and More*. Adapted and illustrated by Harold Berson. New York: Crown, 1974.

—— *Larbi and Leila; a Tale of Two Mice*. New York: Seabury Press, 1974.

Bishop, Claire Huchet. *The Five Chinese Brothers*. Illustrated by Kurt Wiese. New York: Coward-McCann, 1938.

Brown, Marcia. *Dick Whittington and His Cat*. Retold and illustrated by Marcia Brown. New York: Charles Scribner's Sons, 1950.

—— *Stone Soup; an Old Tale*. Told and pictured by Marcia Brown. New York: Charles Scribner's Sons, 1947.

Brown, Margaret Wise. *Goodnight Moon*. Illustrated by Clement Hurd. New York: Harper and Row, 1947.

Buck, Pearl S. *The Chinese Story Teller*. Illustrated by Regina Shekerjian. New York: John Day, 1971.

Buckley, Helen E. *Grandfather and I*. Illustrated by Paul Galdone. New York: Lothrop, Lee & Shepard, 1959.

Buff, Mary and Conrad. *The Arrow and the Apple*. Illustrated by Conrad Buff. Boston: Houghton Mifflin, 1951.

Burton, Virginia Lee. *The Little House*. Illustrated by the author. Boston: Houghton Mifflin, 1942.

—— *Mike Mulligan and His Steam Shovel*. Illustrated by the author. Boston: Houghton Mifflin, 1939.

Carew, Jan. *The Third Gift*. Illustrated by Leo and Diane Dillon. Boston: Little, Brown, 1974.

Caudill, Rebecca. *A Certain Small Shepherd*. Illustrated by Wm. Du Bois. New York: Holt, Rinehart and Winston, 1965.

Chaucer, Geoffrey. *Chanticleer and the Fox*. Adapted and illustrated by Barbara Cooney. New York: Thomas Y. Crowell, 1958.

Daugherty, James. *Andy and the Lion*. Illustrated by the author. New York: Viking Press, 1938.

d'Aulaire, Ingri and Edgar. *D'Aulaires' Trolls*. Garden City, N.Y.: Doubleday, 1972.

De Brunhoff, Jean. *The Story of Babar, the Little Elephant*. Illustrated by the author. Translated from the French by Merle S. Haas. New York: Random House, 1933, 1960.

De Regniers, Beatrice. *May I Bring a Friend?* Illustrated by Beni Montresor. New York: Atheneum, 1964.

Ets, Marie Hall. *Gilberto and the Wind*. Illustrated by the author. New York: Viking Press, 1963.

———— *Play with Me*. Illustrated by the author. New York: Viking Press, 1955.

Fatio, Louise. *The Happy Lion in Africa*. Illustrated by Roger Duvoisin. New York, McGraw-Hill, 1955.

Flack, Marjorie. *Ask Mr. Bear*. Illustrated by the author. New York: Macmillan, 1932.

———— *The Story About Ping*. Illustrated by Kurt Wiese. New York: Viking Press, 1961.

The Fox Went Out on a Chilly Night; an Old Song. Illustrated by Peter Spier. Garden City, N.Y.: Doubleday, 1962.

Freeman, Don. *Come Again, Pelican*. Illustrated by the author. New York: Viking Press, 1961.

Gág, Wanda. *Gone Is Gone, or The Story of a Man Who Wanted to Do Housework*. Retold and illustrated by Wanda Gág. London: Faber & Faber, 1936.

———— *Millions of Cats*. Illustrated by the author. New York: Coward-McCann, 1928.

Ginsburg, Mirra. *The Proud Maiden, Tungak and the Sun*. Illustrated by Igor Galanin. New York: Macmillan, 1974.

Grabianski, Janusz. *Cats*. New York: Franklin Watts, 1967.

Grimm, Jakob Ludwig and Wilhelm Karl. *King Grisly-Beard*. Translated by Edgar Taylor. Illustrated by Maurice Sendak. New York: Farrar, Straus & Giroux, 1973.

—— *Tom Thumb*. Illustrated by Felix Hoffman. New York: Atheneum, 1973.

Haley, Gail E. *A Story, a Story*. Illustrated by the author. New York: Atheneum, 1970.

Hogrogian, Nonny. *One Fine Day*. Retold and illustrated by the author. New York: Macmillan, 1971.

—— *Rooster Brother*. New York: Macmillan, 1974.

Houston, James. *Kiviok's Magic Journey; an Eskimo Legend*. Illustrated by the author. New York: Atheneum, 1973.

Ionesco, Eugene. *Story Number 2, for Children Under Three Years of Age*. Illustrated by Etienne Delessert. New York: Harlin-Quist, 1970.

Jack and the Beanstalk: The History of Mother Twaddle and the Marvelous Achievements of Her Son Jack. Illustrated by Paul Galdone. New York: Seabury Press, 1974.

Jacobs, Joseph. *The Crock of Gold*. A picture book by William Stobbs, being "The Pedlar of Swaffham" by Joseph Jacobs. Chicago: Follett, 1971.

Kahl, Virginia. *The Duchess Bakes a Cake*. Illustrated by the author. New York: Charles Scribner's Sons, 1955.

Keats, Ezra Jack. *Letter to Amy*. Illustrated by the author. New York: Harper and Row, 1968.

—— *The Snowy Day*. Illustrated by the author. New York: Viking Press, 1962.

—— *Whistle for Willie*. Illustrated by the author. New York: Viking Press, 1964.

Kerr, Judith. *Mog the Forgetful Cat*. Illustrated by the author. New York: Parents' Magazine Press, 1972.

Krauss, Ruth. *The Carrot Seed.* Illustrated by Crockett Johnson. New York: Harper & Row, 1945.

———*A Hole Is to Dig.* Illustrated by Maurice Sendak. New York: Harper & Row, 1952.

Langstaff, John. *Over in the Meadow.* Illustrated by Feodor Rojankovsky. New York: Harcourt, Brace and World, 1957.

Leaf, Munro. *The Story of Ferdinand.* Illustrated by Robert Lawson. New York: Viking Press, 1936.

Leichman, Seymour. *The Wicked Wizard, Wicked Witch.* New York: Harcourt Brace Jovanovich, 1972.

Levitin, Sonia. *Who Owns the Moon?* Illustrated by John Larrecq. Berkeley: Parnassus Press, 1973.

Lionni, Leo. *Inch by Inch.* Illustrated by the author. New York: Ivan Obolensky, 1960.

——— *Little Blue and Little Yellow, a Story for Pippo and Ann and Other Children.* Illustrated by the author. New York: McDowell, Obolensky, 1959.

McCloskey, Robert. *Blueberries for Sal.* Illustrated by the author. New York: Viking Press, 1948.

——— *Make Way for Ducklings.* Illustrated by the author. New York: Viking Press, 1969.

——— *Time of Wonder.* Illustrated by the author. New York: Viking Press, 1957.

McDermott, Beverly Brodsky. *The Crystal Apple; a Russian Tale.* Illustrated by the author. New York: Viking Press, 1974.

McDermott, Gerald. *Arrow to the Sun; a Pueblo Indian Tale.* Adapted and illustrated by Gerald McDermott. New York: Viking Press, 1974.

McKee, David. *The Man Who Was Going to Mind the House;*

a Norwegian Folk-tale. Retold and illustrated by David McKee. New York: Abelard-Schuman, 1972.

Merriam, Eve. *Epaminondas*. Retold (from Sara Cone Bryant's story) by Eve Merriam. Illustrated by Trina Schart Hyman. New York: Wm. Collins Sons, 1968.

Munari, Bruno. *A. B. C.* New York: World, 1960.

——— *Bruno Munari's Zoo*. New York: World, 1963.

Ness, Evaline. *Sam, Bangs and Moonshine*. Illustrated by the author. New York: Holt, Rinehart and Winston, 1966.

Numano, Masako. *Dragon, the Rain God; Old Japanese Tale from Konjaku-Monogatari*. Retold and illustrated by Masako Numano. Tokyo: Fukuinkan-Shoten, 1974.

The Old Woman and the Pig. Book designed by Paul Galdone. New York: McGraw-Hill, 1960.

O'Neill, Mary. *Hailstones and Halibut Bones: Adventures in Color*. Illustrated by Leonard Weisgard. Garden City, N.Y.: Doubleday, 1961.

Perrault, Charles. *Cinderella or The Little Glass Slipper*. A free translation from the French of Charles Perrault, with pictures by Marcia Brown. New York: Charles Scribner's Sons, 1954.

——— *Puss in Boots*. A free translation from the French of Charles Perrault, with pictures by Marcia Brown. New York: Charles Scribner's Sons, 1952.

Politi, Leo. *Juanita*. Illustrated by the author. New York: Charles Scribner's Sons, 1948.

——— *Little Leo*. Illustrated by the author. New York: Charles Scribner's Sons, 1951.

——— *Song of the Swallows*. Illustrated by the author. New York: Charles Scribner's Sons, 1948.

Potter, Beatrix. *The Tale of Peter Rabbit*. Illustrated by the author. London: Frederick Warne, n.d.

Prieto, Mariana, and Hopper, Grizella. *Birdmen of Papantla.* Illustrated by Macduff Everton. Los Angeles: Ward Ritchie Press, 1972.

Rey, Hans Augusto. *Curious George.* Illustrated by the author. Boston: Houghton Mifflin, 1969.

Rojankovsky, Feodor. *Animals in the Zoo.* Illustrated by the author. New York: Alfred A. Knopf, 1962.

Sendak, Maurice. *Where the Wild Things Are.* Illustrated by the author. New York: Harper & Row, 1963.

Seta, Teiji. *A Lucky Hunter; an Old Japanese Tale.* Retold by Teiji Seta. Illustrated by Suekichi Akaba. Tokyo: Fukuinkan-Shoten, 1973.

Seuss, Dr. *The 500 Hats of Bartholomew Cubbins.* New York: Vanguard Press, 1938.

Shobenji, Haruko. *The Rainbow Deer; a Story from the Uji Miscellany.* Translated by Ann Herring. Illustrated by Toshi Maruki. Tokyo: Gakken, 1973.

Slobodkina, Esphyr. *Caps for Sale; a Tale of a Peddler, Some Monkeys and Their Monkey Business.* Illustrated by the author. Reading, Mass.: Addison-Wesley, 1947.

Steig, William. *Sylvester and the Magic Pebble.* Illustrated by the author. New York: Simon & Schuster, 1969.

Steptoe, John. *Stevie.* Illustrated by the author. New York: Harper & Row, 1969.

Susanna's Auction. From the French. Illustrated by Boutet de Monvel . . . New York: Macmillan, 1923, 1941.

The Three Bears. Illustrated by Paul Galdone. New York: Seabury Press, 1972.

Thurber, James. *Many Moons.* Illustrated by Louis Slobodkin. New York: Harcourt, Brace, 1943.

Troughton, Joanna. *Sir Gawain and the Loathly Damsel.* Retold and illustrated by Joanna Troughton. New York: E. P. Dutton, 1972.

Wiesner, William. *Turnabout; a Norwegian Tale*. Retold and illustrated by William Wiesner. New York: Seabury Press, 1972.

Wildsmith, Brian. *Brian Wildsmith's A B C*. New York: Oxford University Press, 1962.

————*Brian Wildsmith's Birds*. New York: Franklin Watts, 1967.

————*Brian Wildsmith's Circus*. New York: Franklin Watts, 1970.

Yashima, Mitsu and Taro. *Crow Boy*. Illustrated by the author. New York: Viking Press, 1955.

———— *Plenty to Watch*. Illustrated by Taro Yashima. New York: Viking Press, 1954.

————*Umbrella*. Illustrated by the author. New York: Viking Press, 1958.

Zemach, Harve. *Nail Soup, a Swedish Folk Tale*. Retold by Harve Zemach. Illustrated by the author. Chicago: Follett, 1964.

Zemach, Harve and Margot. *Duffy and the Devil; a Cornish Tale*. Retold by Harve Zemach. Illustrated by Margot Zemach. New York: Farrar, Straus & Giroux, 1973.

Special Poetry

Poetry speaks to everyone but not always in the same key or the same mood or tempo. It is a personal phenomenon, and each storyteller must find poems that speak to him or her, poems with which he or she can identify sufficiently to share them with children. Happily, there are many kinds of poetry from which to choose. This is a sampling to be explored.

Adoff, Arnold, comp. *I Am the Darker Brother; an Anthology of Modern Poems by Negro Americans*. Illustrated by Benny Andrews . . . New York: Macmillan, 1968.

Allen, Terry, ed. *The Whispering Wind; Poetry by Young American Indians*. Introduction by Mae J. Durham. Garden City, N.Y.: Doubleday, 1972.

Arbuthnot, May Hill. *Time for Poetry*. Chicago: Scott, Foresman, 1961.

Association for Childhood Education International. *Sung Under the Silver Umbrella*. Illustrated by Dorothy P. Lathrop. New York: Macmillan, 1972.

Atwood, Ann. *Haiku; the Mood of Earth*. Photographs by the author. New York: Charles Scribner's Sons, 1971.

Behn, Harry. *Cricket Songs; Japanese Haiku*. New York: Harcourt, Brace, 1964.

_____ *The Little Hill; Poems and Pictures* . . . New York: Harcourt, Brace and World, 1949.

Benét, Stephen Vincent and Rosemary. *A Book of Americans*. Illustrated by Charles Child. New York: Holt, Rinehart and Winston, 1933, 1961.

Blishen, Edward, comp. *Oxford Book of Poetry for Children*. Illustrated by Brian Wildsmith. New York: Franklin Watts, 1963.

Bonner, Ann and Roger. *Earlybirds . . . Earlywords*. New York: Scroll Press, 1973.

Bouton, Josephine, comp. *Favorite Poems for the Children's Hour*. Illustrated by Bonnie and Bill Rutherford . . . New York: Platt & Munk, 1967.

Brecht, Bertolt. *Uncle Eddie's Moustache; Twelve Poems for Children*. Translated by Muriel Rukeyser. Illustrated by Ursula Kirchberg. New York: Pantheon Books, 1974.

Brewton, John E., comp. *Under the Tent of the Sky; a Collection of Poems About Animals Large and Small*. Illustrated by Robert Lawson. New York: Macmillan, 1937.

Brewton, Sara and John E., and Blackburn, G. Meredith III, comps. *My Tang's Tungled and Other Ridiculous Situations; Humorous Poems.* Illustrated by Graham Booth. New York: Thomas Y. Crowell, 1973.

Burns, Robert. *Hand in Hand We'll Go; Ten Poems by Robert Burns.* Illustrated by Nonny Hogrogian. New York: Thomas Y. Crowell, 1965.

Carroll, Lewis. *The Walrus and the Carpenter.* Illustrated by Tony Cattaneo. New York: Frederick Warne, 1975.

Causley, Charles. *As I Went Down Zig Zag.* Illustrated by John Astrop. New York: Frederick Warne, 1975.

_____ *Figgie Hobbin.* Illustrated by Trina Schart Hyman. Introduction by Ethel L. Heins. New York: Walker, 1973.

Chute, Marchette. *Around and About; Rhymes.* Illustrated by the author. New York: E. P. Dutton, 1957.

Ciardi, John. *The Man Who Sang the Sillies.* Illustrated by Edward Gorey. Philadelphia: Lippincott, 1961.

Cole, William, comp. *Oh, That's Ridiculous!* . . . Illustrated by Tomi Ungerer. New York: Viking Press, 1972.

_____, ed. *Pick Me Up; a Book of Short Short Poems.* New York: Macmillan, 1972.

Cummings, E. E. *A Selection of Poems* . . . New York: Harcourt, Brace and World, 1923, 1965.

de Angeli, Marguerite. *Book of Nursery and Mother Goose Rhymes.* Garden City, N.Y.: Doubleday, 1954.

De la Mare, Walter. *Come Hither; A Collection of Rhymes and Poems for the Young of All Ages.* Illustrated by Diana Bloomfield. New York: Alfred A. Knopf, 1957.

_____ *Poems for Children.* New York: Henry Holt, 1930.

Dunning, Stephen, and others. *Reflections on a Gift of Watermelon Pickle . . . and Other Modern Verse.* Glenview, Ill.: Scott, Foresman, 1966.

Eliot, T. S. *Old Possum's Book of Practical Cats*. London: Faber & Faber, 1939.

Emrich, Duncan, comp. *The Nonsense Book of Riddles, Rhymes, Tongue Twisters, Puzzles and Jokes from American Folklore*. Illustrated by Ib Ohlsson. New York: Four Winds Press, 1970.

Ferris, Helen, comp. *Favorite Poems Old and New, Selected for Boys and Girls*. Illustrated by Leonard Weisgard. Garden City, N.Y.: Doubleday, 1957.

Field, Rachel. *Poems*. Illustrated by the author. New York: Macmillan, 1957.

Fisher, Aileen. *In the Middle of the Night*. Illustrated by Adrienne Adams. New York: Thomas Y. Crowell, 1965.

Frost, Robert. *You Come Too; Favorite Poems for Young Readers*. Illustrated by Thomas W. Nason. New York: Holt, Rinehart and Winston, 1959.

Fyleman, Rose. *Fairies and Chimneys*. New York: George H. Doran, 1920.

——— *Nursery Rhymes from Many Lands*. Translated by Rose Fyleman. Illustrated by Valery Carrick. New York: Dover, 1971.

Gerez, Toni De. *2–Rabbit, 7–Wind; Poems from Ancient Mexico*. Retold from Nahuatl texts. New York: Viking Press, 1971.

Giovanni, Nikki. *Ego-tripping and Other Poems for Young People*. Illustrated by George Ford. New York: Hill and Wang, 1973.

——— *Spin a Soft Black Song*. Illustrated by Charles Bible. New York: Hill and Wang, 1971.

Greenaway, Kate. *Mother Goose or the Old Nursery Rhymes*. Illustrated by Kate Greenaway. London: Frederick Warne, n.d.

Gregg, Ernest. *And the Sun God Said: That's Hip.* Illustrated by G. Falcon Beazer. New York: Harper & Row, 1972.

Hardy, Thomas. *The Pinnacled Tower: Selected Poems of Thomas Hardy.* Edited by Helen Plotz. Illustrated by Clare Leighton. New York: Macmillan, 1975.

Hazeltine, Alice I. and Smith, Elva S., comps. *The Year Around; Poems for Children.* Illustrated by Paula Hutchison. New York: Abingdon Press, 1956.

Hoberman, Mary Ann. *The Raucous Auk; a Menagerie of Poems.* Illustrated by Joseph Low. New York: Viking Press, 1973.

Hopkins, Lee, comp. *Me! A Book of Poems.* Illustrated by Tativaldis Stubis. New York: Seabury Press, 1970.

———— *Zoo! A Book of Poems.* Illustrated by Robert Frankenberg. New York: Crown, 1971.

Hughes, Langston. *Don't You Turn Back . . .* Selected by Lee Bennett Hopkins. Illustrated by Ann Grifalconi. New York: Alfred A. Knopf, 1969.

———— *The Dream Keeper and Other Poems.* Illustrated by Helen Sewell. New York: Alfred A. Knopf, 1932.

Jordan, June, and Bush, Terri, comps. *The Voice of the Children.* New York: Holt, Rinehart and Winston, 1970.

Kaufman, William I., comp. *UNICEF Book of Children's Poems.* Compiled and with photographs by William I. Kaufman. Adapted for English-reading children by Joan Gilbert Van Poznak. Harrisburg, Pa.: Stackpole Books, 1970.

Larrick, Nancy, comp. *Green Is Like a Meadow of Grass; an Anthology of Children's Pleasure in Poetry.* Selected by Nancy Larrick. Illustrated by Kelly Oechsli. Champaign, Ill.: Garrard, 1968.

——— *I Heard a Scream in the Street; Poems by Young People in the City*. Illustrated with photographs by students. New York: M. Evans, 1970.

Lear, Edward. *The Complete Nonsense of Edward Lear*. Edited and with an introduction by Holbrook Jackson. Illustrated by the author. New York: Dover, 1951.

Lenski, Lois. *City Poems*. New York: Henry Z. Walck, 1971.

Lewis, Richard, ed. *In a Spring Garden*. Illustrated by Ezra Jack Keats. New York: Dial Press, 1965.

——— *There Are Two Lives; Poems by Children of Japan*. Translated by Haruna Kimura. New York: Simon & Schuster, 1970.

Livingston, Myra Cohn. *Come Away*. Illustrated by Irene Haas. New York: Atheneum, 1974.

———, ed. *Listen, Children, Listen; an Anthology of Poems for the Very Young*. Illustrated by Trina Schart Hyman. New York: Harcourt, Brace and World, 1972.

———*A Tune Beyond Us; a Collection of Poetry*. New York: Harcourt, Brace and World, 1968.

——— *The Way Things Are; and Other Poems*. Illustrated by Jenni Oliver. New York: Atheneum, 1974.

McCord, David. *All Day Long; Fifty Rhymes of the Never Was and Always Is*. Illustrated by Henry B. Kane. New York: Dell, 1965.

——— *Every Time I Climb a Tree*. Illustrated by Marc Simont. Boston: Little, Brown, 1967.

McEwen, Catherine Schaefer, comp. *Away We Go! 100 Poems for the Very Young*. Illustrated by Barbara Cooney. New York: Thomas Y. Crowell, 1956.

McGee, Barbara, comp. *Jump-Rope Rhymes*. Collected and illustrated by Barbara McGee. New York: Viking Press, 1968.

Merriam, Eve. *It Doesn't Always Have to Rhyme*. New York: Atheneum, 1964.

———— *Out Loud*. New York: Atheneum, 1973.

———— *There Is No Rhyme for Silver*. New York: Atheneum, 1962.

Millay, Edna St. Vincent. *Edna St. Vincent Millay's Poems Selected for Young People*. Illustrated by J. Paget-Fredericks. New York: Harper & Brothers, 1929.

Milne, Alan Alexander. *Now We Are Six*. Illustrated by E. H. Shepard. London: Methuen, 1927.

———— *When We Were Very Young*. Illustrated by E. H. Shepard. New York: E. P. Dutton, 1966.

Montgomerie, Norah and William. *A Book of Scottish Nursery Rhymes*. Collected and edited by Norah and William Montgomerie. Illustrated by T. Ritchie and N. Montgomerie. New York: Oxford University Press, 1964.

Mother Goose. *Mother Goose Lost; Nursery Rhymes*. Collected by Nicholas Tucker. Illustrated by Trevor Stubley. New York: Thomas Y. Crowell, 1971.

Nash, Ogden, comp. *The Moon Is Shining Bright as Day; an Anthology of Good-Humored Verse*. Selected, with an introduction by Ogden Nash. Illustrated by Rose Shirvanian. Philadelphia: J. B. Lippincott, 1953.

O'Neill, Mary. *People I'd Like to Keep*. Illustrated by Paul Galdone. Garden City, N.Y.: Doubleday, 1964.

———— *Words, Words, Words*. Illustrated by Judy Piussi-Campbell. Garden City, N.Y.: Doubleday, 1966.

Opie, Iona and Peter. *The Puffin Book of Nursery Rhymes*. Illustrated by Pauline Baynes. Baltimore: Penguin Books, 1963.

Palmer, Geoffrey. *Round About Eight; Poems of Today*. Selected by Geoffrey Palmer and Noel Lord. Illustrated by

Denis Wrigley. New York: Frederick Warne, 1972.

Payne, Nina. *All the Day Long.* Illustrated by Laurel Schindelman. New York: Atheneum, 1973.

Plotz, Helen. *Imagination's Other Place; Poems of Science and Mathematics.* New York: Thomas Y. Crowell, 1955.

_____ *Untune the Sky; Poems of Music and the Dance.* New York: Thomas Y. Crowell, 1957.

Regniers, Beatrice Schenck de; Moore, Eva; and White, Mary Michaels, comps. *Poems That Children Will Sit Still For.* New York: Citation Press, 1969.

Richards, Laura E. *Tirra Lirra; Rhymes Old and New . . .* Illustrated by Marguerite Davis. Boston: Little, Brown, 1955.

Roethke, Theodore. *Dirty Dinky and Other Creatures; Poems for Children.* Selected by Beatrice Roethke and Stephen Lushington. Garden City, N.Y.: Doubleday, 1973.

Sandburg, Carl. *Early Moon.* Illustrated by James Daugherty. New York: Harcourt, Brace, 1930.

_____ *Wind Song.* Illustrated by William A. Smith. New York: Harcourt, Brace & World, 1960.

Smith, William Jay. *Boy Blue's Book of Beasts.* Illustrated by Juliet Kepes. Boston: Little, Brown, 1957.

Snyder, Zilpha Keatley. *Today Is Saturday.* Photographs by John Arms. New York: Atheneum, 1969.

Stevenson, Robert Louis. *A Child's Garden of Verses.* Illustrated by Brian Wildsmith. New York: Franklin Watts, 1966.

Summerfield, Geoffrey, ed. *First Voices; the First Book.* New York: Alfred A. Knopf and Random House, 1970.

Swift, Hildegarde Hoyt. *North Star Shining; a Pictorial History of the American Negro.* Illustrated by Lynd Ward. New York: William Morrow, 1947.

Tashjian, Virginia A., comp. *Juba This and Juba That; Story*

Hour Stretches for Large or Small Groups. Illustrated by Victoria de Larrea. Boston: Little, Brown, 1969.

_____ *With a Deep Sea Smile; Story Hour Stretches for Large or Small Groups.* Selected by Virginia Tashjian. Illustrated by Rosemary Wells. Boston: Little, Brown, 1974.

Thompson, Blanche Jennings, ed. *All the Silver Pennies* (combining *Silver Pennies* and *More Silver Pennies*). Illustrated by Ursula Arndt. New York: Macmillan, 1967.

Tudor, Tasha, comp. *Mother Goose.* Illustrated by Tasha Tudor. New York: Oxford University Press, 1944.

Untermeyer, Louis, comp. and ed. *The Golden Book of Fun and Nonsense.* Illustrated by A. and M. Provensen. New York: Golden Press, 1970.

_____ *The Magic Circle: Stories and People in Poetry.* Illustrated by Beth and Joe Krush. New York: Harcourt, Brace, 1952.

Watson, Clyde. *Father Fox's Pennyrhymes.* Illustrated by Wendy Watson. New York: Thomas Y. Crowell, 1971.

Worstell, Emma V., ed. *Jump the Rope Jingles.* Abridged edition. Illustrated by Sheila Greenwald. New York: Macmillan, 1972.

WHAT TO READ TO IMPROVE YOUR SKILL

Books on voice and speech improvement, oral interpretation of literature, choral speaking, finger plays, creative dramatics, and puppetry—all these I have grouped together as works designed to improve your artistry in storytelling. There is some overlapping among them. A book dealing with oral interpretation of literature frequently covers such topics as choral speaking, voice improvement, and even creative dramatics. I have tried to place each book into one specific group as far as possible, but you will find useful ideas in all of the books listed.

Voice and Speech

Akin, Johnnye. *And So We Speak; Voice and Articulation.* Englewood Cliffs, N.J.: Prentice-Hall, 1958.

Auer, J. Jeffery, and Jenkinson, Edward P., eds. *On Teaching Speech in Elementary and Junior High Schools . . .* Bloomington: Indiana University Press, 1971.

Avery, Elizabeth, and others. *First Principles of Speech Training* by Elizabeth Avery, Jane Dorsey, and Vera A. Sickels . . . New York: Appleton-Century-Crofts, 1928, 1956.

Bordeaux, Jean. *How to Talk More Effectively.* With the collaboration of T. W. Tanaka. Revised by Susan Z. Diamond. Chicago: American Technical Society, 1973.

Fairbanks, Grant. *Voice and Articulation Drillbook.* 2nd edition. New York: Harper & Row, 1960.

Fisher, Hilda B. *Improving Voice and Articulation.* Boston: Houghton Mifflin, 1966.

Huckleberry, Alan W., and Strother, Edward S. *Speech Education for the Elementary Teacher.* Boston: Allyn and Bacon, 1966.

Lessac, Arthur. *The Use and Training of the Human Voice; A Practical Approach to Speech and Voice Dynamics.* New York: Drama Book Shop, 1967.

McBurney, James H. and Wrage, Ernest J. *Guide to Good Speech.* 3rd edition. Englewood Cliffs, N.J.: Prentice-Hall, 1965.

Quick, John. *I Hate to Make Speeches—Help for People Who Must.* Illustrated by Larry Kirby. New York: Grosset & Dunlap, 1973.

Wentworth, Harold. *American Dialect Dictionary*. New York: Thomas Y. Crowell, 1944.

Oral Interpretation

Bacon, Wallace A. *The Art of Interpretation*. 2nd edition. New York: Holt, Rinehart and Winston, 1972.

Bamman, Henry A. and others. *Oral Interpretation of Children's Literature* . . . Illustrated by Tony Flores. Dubuque, Iowa: Wm. C. Brown, 1964.

Lee, Charlotte I. *Oral Interpretation*. 4th edition. Boston: Houghton Mifflin, 1971.

Lowrey, Sara, and Johnson, Gertrude E. . . . *Interpretative Reading: Techniques and Selections*. Revised edition. New York: Appleton-Century-Crofts, 1953.

Choral Speaking

Gullan, Marjorie. *Choral Speaking*. 3rd revised edition. New York: Barnes & Noble, 1936.

_____ *The Speech Choir; with American Poetry and English Ballads for Choral Reading*. New York: Harper, 1937.

_____ *Spoken Poetry in the Schools* . . . 6th edition. New York: Barnes & Noble, 1935.

Keppie, Elizabeth Evangeline, and others. *Speech Improvement Through Choral Speaking, a Textbook for Teachers of Primary Grades* . . . Boston: Expression, 1942.

_____ *The Teaching of Choric Speech* . . . Boston: Expression, n.d.

Finger Plays

Glazer, Tom. *Eye Winker, Tom Tinker, Chin Chopper; Fifty*

Musical Finger Plays (with piano arrangements and guitar chords). Illustrated by Ron Himler. Garden City, N.Y.: Doubleday, 1973.

Grayson, Marion. *Let's Do Finger Plays*. Illustrated by Nancy Weyl. Washington, D.C.: Robert B. Luce, 1962.

Hogstrom, Daphne. *Little Boy Blue, Finger Plays Old and New*. Illustrated by Alice Schlesinger. New York: Whitman, 1966.

Matterson, Elizabeth, comp. *Games for the Very Young; Finger Plays and Nursery Games*. New York: American Heritage Press, 1969.

Montgomerie, Nora, comp. *This Little Pig Went to Market; Play Rhymes*. Illustrated by Margery Gill. New York: Franklin Watts, 1966.

Nakagawa, Masafumi. *Hand Shadows*. Illustrated by Hiroshi Akana. Tokyo: Fukuinkan-Shoten, 1970.

Scott, Louise Binder, and Thompson, J. J. *Rhymes for Fingers and Flannel Boards*. Illustrated by Jean Flowers. New York: McGraw-Hill, 1960.

Yamaguchi, Marianne. *Finger Plays*. Illustrated by the author. New York: Holt, Rinehart and Winston, 1972.

Creative Dramatics

Byers, Ruth. *Creating Theatre; from Idea Through Performance with Children and Teens*. San Antonio: Trinity University Press, 1968.

Carlson, Bernice. *Funny Bone Dramatics*. Illustrated by Charles Cox. Nashville: Abingdon Press, 1974.

_____ *Listen! And Help Tell the Story*. Illustrated by Burmah Burris. Nashville, Abingdon Press, 1965.

Cheifetz, Dan. *Theatre in My Head* (How children learn and

grow through dramatic play.) Photographs by Nancy Hellebrand. Boston: Little, Brown, 1971.

Crosscup, Richard. *Children and Dramatics*. New York: Charles Scribner's Sons, 1966.

Cullum, Albert. *Aesop in the Afternoon; 65 Playlets Adapted from the Fables*. New York: Citation Press, 1972.

Fitzgerald, Burdett S. *Let's Act the Story; a Leader's Guide for Dramatic Fun with Children's Literature*. San Francisco: Fearon, 1957.

_____, comp. *World Tales for Creative Dramatics and Storytelling*. Englewood Cliffs, N.J.: Prentice-Hall, 1962.

Goodridge, Janet. *Creative Drama and Improvised Movement for Children*. Boston: Plays, 1970.

Kamerman, Sylvia. *Children's Plays from Favorite Stories*. Boston: Plays, 1970.

Kerman, Gertrude Lerner. *Plays and Creative Ways with Children*. New York: Harvey House, 1961.

McSweeny, Maxine. *Creative Children's Theatre for Home, School, Church, and Playground*. New York: A. S. Barnes, 1974.

Siks, Geraldine Brain. *Children's Literature for Dramatization; an Anthology*. New York: Harper & Row, 1964.

_____and Dunnington, Hazel Brain, eds. *Theatre and Creative Dramatics*. Seattle: University of Washington Press, 1961.

Walker, Pamela Prince. *Seven Steps to Creative Children's Dramatics*. New York: Hill and Wang, 1957.

Ward, Winifred. *Playmaking with Children from Kindergarten to High School*. New York: Appleton-Century, 1947.

_____*Stories to Dramatize*. Anchorage, Ky.: Children's Theatre Press, 1952.

Puppetry

Adair, Margaret Weeks. *Do-It-In-A-Day Puppets; for Beginners* . . . New York: John Day, 1964.

——and Patapoff, Elizabeth. *Folk Puppet Plays for the Social Studies.* New York: John Day, 1972.

Alkema, Chester Jay. *Puppet-Making.* (Little Craft Book Series) New York: Sterling, 1971. 2nd printing, 1972.

Boylan, Eleanor. *How to Be a Puppeteer.* Illustrated by Tomie de Paola. New York: McCall, 1970.

Engler, Larry. *Making Puppets Come Alive; a Method of Teaching Hand Puppetry* by Larry Engler and Carol Fijan. Photography by David Attie . . . New York: Taplinger, 1973.

Lewis, Shari. *Making Easy Puppets.* Illustrated by Larry Lurin. New York: E. P. Dutton, 1967.

Rasmussen, Carrie, and Storck, Caroline. *Fun-Time Puppets.* Illustrated by Caroline Storck. Chicago: Children's Press, 1952.

Ross, Laura. *Finger Puppets; Easy to Make, Fun to Use.* Illustrated by Laura and Frank Ross, Jr. New York: Lothrop, Lee & Shepard, 1971.

——*Hand Puppets; How to Make Them and Use Them.* Illustrated by the author. New York: Lothrop, Lee & Shepard, 1969.

——*Holiday Puppets* by Laura Ross. Drawings and diagrams by Frank and Laura Ross. New York: Lothrop, Lee, & Shepard, 1974.

——*Puppet Shows, Using Poems and Stories.* Illustrated by Frank Ross, Jr. New York: Lothrop, Lee & Shepard, 1970.

Worrell, Estelle Ansley. *Be a Puppeteer!* New York: McGraw-Hill, 1969.

WHAT TO USE FOR LANGUAGE DIFFERENCES

As the language needs of ethnic minorities have become increasingly recognized, publishers have undertaken to issue bilingual, multilingual, and foreign-language story and picture books. The storyteller who is himself bilingual is fortunate indeed, for he can create a genuine rapport with listeners who share his special language. The storyteller who is not bilingual but who wants to use such books can learn the words and sounds that give the stories a distinctive quality. It is much more difficult to comprehend the nuances of the ethnic cultures, but a sympathetic concern will come through with the use of bilingual materials.

Children's books have been produced all over the world as can be seen by examining Anne Pellowski's bibliography (see p. 122); good bilingual books as well as English language stories translated into foreign languages are now becoming more accessible. In addition to a number of bilingual stories and picture books, I have included some stories that have been translated from English into a foreign language. This enables the storyteller to use a foreign language book and its English counterpart in one story hour program.

These are a few of available materials. If you are in a bilingual or multilingual community, I suggest you visit your local or school library to ascertain what and how many bilingual or foreign-language books are available for your needs.

Danish Language Books

Andersen, Hans Christian. *Tommelise* ("Thumbelina"). Illustrated by Kaj Beckman. Copenhagen: Gyldendal, 1967.

Ness, Evaline. *Sam, Bum og Pølsesnak* ("Sam, Bangs, and Moonshine"). På dansk ved Inge og Klaus Rifberg. Copenhagen Bookprint, 1968.

French Language Books

Aesop. *Le Meunier, son fils, et l'âne* ("The Farmer, His Sons, and the Donkey"). Illustration et traduction de Roger Duvoisin. New York: Whittlesey House, 1962.

Anglund, Joan Walsh. *Un Ami, c'est quelqu'un qui t'aime* ("A Friend Is Someone Who Loves You"). Traduit par Anne Carter. New York: Harcourt, Brace & World, 1965.

Barret, Judi. *Il ne faut pas habiller les animaux* ("The Animals Need No Clothes"). Illustrated by Ron Barrett. Paris: L'École des Loisirs, 1971.

Fatio, Louise. *Le Bon Lion* ("The Happy Lion"). Dessin de Roger Duvoisin. Tours, France: Maison Mame, 1954.

Lionni, Leo. *La Maison la plus grande du monde* ("The Biggest House in the World"). Illustrated by Leo Lionni. Paris: L'École des Loisirs, 1971.

Mother Goose. *Mother Goose in French*. Translated by Hugh Latham. Illustrated by Barbara Cooney. New York: Thomas Y. Crowell, 1964.

Potter, Beatrix. *L'Histoire de Pierre Lapin* ("The Story of Peter Rabbit"). Traduit de l'anglais par Victorine Ballon & Julienne Profichet. New York: Frederick Warne, 1973.

Steegmuller, Francis. *Le Hibou et la poussiquette* ("The Owl and the Pussycat"). Illustrated by Barbara Cooney. Boston: Little, Brown, 1959.

German Language Books

Fatio, Louise. *Zwei Glückliche Löwen* ("The Happy Lion"). Gemalt von Roger Duvoisin. Übersetzt von Fritz Muhlenveg. Germany: Herder-Druck Freiburg im Breisgau, 1958.

Stevenson, Robert Louis. *Im Versgarten; Gedichte für ein Kind* ("A Child's Garden of Verses"). Ein Bilderbuch von A. und M. Provenson. Mit Versen von Robert Louis Stevenson ins Deutsche übertragen von James Krüss . . . New York: Simon & Schuster, 1957.

Italian Language Books

Potter, Beatrix. *Il Coniglio Pierino* ("Peter Rabbit"). Tradotta in Italiano da R. C. Ruggieri. London: Frederick Warne, n.d.

Japanese Language Books

Hanada, Yaichi. *Ringo* ("Apples"). Illustrated by the author. Tokyo: Fukuinkan-Shoten, 1972.

Iwasaki, Kyoko. *Yowamushi na Jitensha* ("The Scaredy-cat Bike"). Illustrated by Ryohei Hosaka. Tokyo: Fukuinkan-Shoten, 1974.

Kitamura, Eri. *Koguma no Taro* ("Little Bear Taro"). Tokyo: Fukuinkan-Shoten, 1973.

Yashima, Taro. *Umbrella*. Translated by the author into Japanese and illustrated by the author. New York: Viking Press, 1970.

Japanese-English Books

Beach, Stewart. *Good Morning, Sun's Up*. Illustrated by Yutaka Sugita. New York: Scroll Press, 1970.

Matsutani, Miyoko. *How the Withered Trees Blossomed*. Illustrated by Yasuo Segawa. Philadelphia: J. B. Lippincott, 1969.

Wakana, Kei. *The Magic Hat*. Illustrated by the author. New York: Scroll Press, 1970.

Russian Language Books

Milne, Alan Alexander. *Vinni-Pukh i vse-vse-vse* ("Winnie-the-Pooh and All-in-All"). A Russian translation by Boris Zakhoder of A. A. Milne's *Winnie the Pooh & The House at Pooh Corner*. Illustrated by B. Diodorov & G. Kelinovsky. New York: E. P. Dutton, 1967.

Spanish Language Books

Andersen, Hans Christian. *Cuatro Cuentos de Andersen* ("Four Stories of Andersen"). Barcelona: Editorial Timun Mas, 1969.

Curry, Nancy. *La Señora Jones es mi Amiga* ("Mrs. Jones Is My Friend"). Fotografías por Harvey Mandlin. Traducción y adaptación por Emma Holquin Jiménez y Conchita Morales Puncel. Glendale, Calif.: Bowmar, 1969.

De Brunhoff, Jean. *El Viaje de Babar* ("Babar's Travels"). Barcelona: Aymá, 1965.

Hoff, Syd. *Danielito y el Dinosauro* ("Andy and the Dinosaur"). Illus. por Syd Hoff. (A Spanish I CAN READ BOOK) Translated from English by Pura Belpré. New York: Harper & Row, 1969.

Leaf, Munro. *El Cuento de Ferdinando* ("The Story of Ferdinand"). Tr. del inglés por Pura Belpré. Illus. por Robert Lawson. New York: Viking Press, 1962.

Lenski, Lois. *La Granja Pequeña* ("The Small Farm"). Translated from English into Spanish by Sandra Streepy. New York: Henry Z. Walck, 1968.

Mother Goose. *Mother Goose in Spanish*. Translated by Alastair Reed and Anthony Kerrigan. Illustrated by Barbara Cooney. New York: Thomas Y. Crowell, 1968.

Potter, Beatrix. *Pedrin: El Conejo Travieso* ("The Story of Peter Rabbit"). London & New York: Frederick Warne, n.d.

Spanish-English Books

Dana, Doris. *The Elephant and His Secret; El Elefante y Su Secreto*. Based on a fable by Gabriela Mistral, in Spanish and English. Illustrated by Antonio Frasconi. New York: Atheneum, 1974.

Jiménez, Emma Holquin, and Puncel, Conchita Morales. *Para Chiquitines; Cáncioncitas, Versitos y Juegos Meñiques* ("Songs, Verses, and Finger Plays"). Illustrated by Gilbert T. Martinez. Glendale, Calif.: Bowmar, 1969.

Lenski, Lois. *Vaquero Pequeño, Cowboy Small*. Spanish translation by Donald Worcester. Illustrated by the author. New York: Henry Z. Walck, 1960.

Rey, Hans Augosto. *Jorge el Curioso* ("Curious George"). Translated into Spanish for young readers by Pedro Villa Fernandez. Boston: Houghton Mifflin, 1941, 1961.

Rider, Alex. *When We Go to School/Cuando Vamos a la Escuela* ... Illustrated by Peter Madden. (Learn a Language Book). New York: Funk & Wagnalls, 1967.

Serfozo, Mary. *Welcome Roberto!!/Bienvenido, Roberto!!* Photographs by John Serfozo. Chicago: Follett, 1969.

Williams, Letty. *The Little Red Hen/La Pequeña Gallina Roja*. Illustrated by Herb Williams. Translated by Doris Chávez and Ed Allen. Englewood Cliffs, N.J.: Prentice-Hall, 1969.

Swedish Language Books

Milne, Alan Alexander. *Nalle Puh, en Hopp-upp Bilderbok* ("Winnie the Pooh, a Pop-up Picture Book"). Bearb av A. Schenk efter original illustrationer av E. H. Shepard. No publisher.

Multilingual Books

Hautzig, Esther. *At Home: A Visit in Four Languages* (English, French, Spanish, Russian). Illustrated by Aliki. New York: Macmillan, 1968.

STORIES FOR MATURER CHILDREN

There are no stories that cannot be told artfully. Some, however, are more difficult than others; some are more suitable to a certain occasion or audience. There is no substitute for good taste and discretion. This is probably best observed in the use of certain picture books. Despite their appearance, which at first glance resembles the usual picture book, the theme and vocabulary of some books are far too sophisticated to be of interest to, or within the comprehension of, immature children. Such books, nevertheless, may be wonderful for older boys and girls. They should be reserved for a time and place that permit informal discussion of the personal problems involved. Even certain books written by children, such as *I Never Saw Another Butterfly* (categorized as a "children's picture-poetry book"), are strong fare for most young appetites. Introduced carefully to special or mature children, they can be very moving and thought-provoking. The storyteller must use them selectively and discreetly.

The books listed here are examples of such "children's" stories and poems. As a storyteller, you should know these books yourself and learn when and with whom to use them.

Alexander, Lloyd. *The King's Fountain*. Illustrated by Ezra Jack Keats. New York: E. P. Dutton, 1971.

Bishop, Elizabeth. *The Ballad of the Burglar of Babylon*. Illustrated by Ann Grifalconi. New York: Farrar, Straus & Giroux, 1968.

Galdone, Paul. *Androcles and the Lion*. Adapted and illustrated by Paul Galdone. New York: McGraw-Hill, 1970.

Hosford, Dorothy. *By His Own Might; the Battles of Beowulf*. Illustrated by Laszlo Matulay. New York: Holt, Rinehart and Winston, 1947.

Jarrell, Randall. *The Animal Family*. Illustrated by Maurice Sendak. New York: Pantheon Books, 1965.

Lawrence, Jacob. *Harriet and the Promised Land*. Illustrated by the author. New York: Simon & Schuster, 1968.

Otsuka, Yuzo. *Suho and the White Horse; a Legend of Mongolia*. Translated by Hirawa Yasuko. Illustrated by Suekichi Akaba. New York: Bobbs-Merrill, n.d.

Terezin Concentration Camp, Prague. *I Never Saw Another Butterfly; Children's Drawings and Poems from Terezin Concentration Camp, 1942–1944*. New York: McGraw-Hill. Printed in Czechoslovakia, n.d.

Weik, Mary Hays. *The Jazz Man*. Illustrated by Ann Grifalconi. New York: Atheneum, 1966.

INDEX

Page numbers in **bold face** indicate material quoted in text.